@ THE STEERING WHEEL OF LIFE

SUCCESS SCRIPTS

Dexter John Valles

Author : Dexter John Valles
Title : @ the Steering Wheel of Life : Success Scripts
Category : Inspiration & Personal Growth, Success, Motivation
Inspired by : The Holy Spirit

First Edition May 2020

DEDICATION

This book is dedicated to

My beloved wife
Maria P Valles
&
My darling daughter
Valerie Anne Valles

NOTE FROM THE AUTHOR

This book is a collection of the more significant articles I have been writing over time.

These have been compiled to offer the reader an opportunity to design a personal success script after learning from the insights in each article.

No Success Script is final and absolute. Each one must write and rewrite their scripts to meet the changing times and life experiences while steering the ship of their lives across the seas and oceans of change.

These articles are handpicked to bring some relief to that quest.

Don't forget to enjoy the journey. Be kind to yourself along the way.

CONTENTS

INTRODUCTION
ASPIRE FOR SUCCESS !
MAKE YOUR ASPIRATIONS A LIFE MISSION

I have come across several articles and books on "Success" and all of them have very special messages for the reader. It is truly motivating to read and learn how people are making their dreams take shape. We can certainly benefit from the lessons learned by those who have driven themselves on the road to success and read the milestones they have placed along the way there, for inscribed on each are invaluable insights of life.

To achieve anything noteworthy in life calls for a certain amount of "stretch" which put plainly means that one has to "struggle" with the performance and delivery of results that meet higher standards that those in play. I would rather call this a raising of the bar or an aspiration in action. Performing within our capabilities guarantees delivery against promises made, but these are mediocre performances delivering mediocre goals. Satisfaction with this leads to a dull sense of happy mediocrity and diminished dreams.

At, Valmar International , where I am the Managing Consultant, we have put together our own definition of success in our Vision Statement, drawing from all those lessons others have learned and shared and our own experiences and aspirations for success. Allow me to share this with you, as we have found these simple truths of life very useful.

We look at adopting these tenets of life as we A-S-P-I-R-E for success learning Six Shining Lessons of Life

A : Accountability for Results

Ownership of the task along with responsibility for performance is a prime element of success. Effort no matter how earnest, without focus or direction cannot deliver excellence. "If it has to be, it's up to me !" is a common enough phrase, but we need to get it off the page and into our work ethic. Desire without a will, subscription to excellence without action, and action without accountability together deliver shallow performances and empty dreams.

The First Lesson here is "Make Your Life Count when You Put Your Signature to it"

S : Strength and Stability of Values

The guide-ropes across life are woven with the values we bring along with us. Values with hold us accountable not just for what we do, but how we do things too. Values contribute to a life with honor and morality. Values provide the higher ground, on which we can breathe the purity of the air of accomplishment, instead of suffocating in the sulphuric swamps of dishonorable practices.

Good corporate governance at the organizational level and personal ethics at the individual level can help create a single transparent and honest agenda of action.

Not having to watch your back or cover your rear while you are engaged in delivering excellence, is a major relief and allows everyone to commit resources without any reservation. Standing firm on what you believe in allows you to advocate your position and interest soundly It's not about being obstinate, but about being definite.

The Second Lesson is "Stamp Goodness on the Charter of Life in Whatever You Do. Seal Life's Envelope with Greatness and Leave Pettiness Penniless"

P : Passion and Purpose in Performance

Consider this. You visit a well promoted township and see towers, buildings, parks, restaurants, shopping malls, schools, hospitals and all that makes a township strewn across the landscape with no apparent design or town planning. You further notice that many of the structures were only partially complete, some surrounded by dense brush and overgrown wasteland whilst some with pruned lawns. Roads run smartly through the town but some abruptly end in rough mounds of rubble. Restaurants run glitzy advertisements of their fare and entertainment programs, but this is only in print and not in practice. Hospitals gleam with the most professional equipment but the medical services are run by it's lone pharmacy dispensing OTC medicines.

You quiz some of the townsfolk about these strange to bizarre matters, and find that they do not sense anything amiss!!

Do we recognize our lives in this context too ? How often do we really plan the township of our life ? Giving in to the flavour of the moment we may develop competences that die faster than they are used, redirect our focus mindlessly into convoluted and often unfinished paths, build towers of performance without the support structure in place, leave the "insignificant balance" of competence, performance, values and relationships unfinished or half constructed for completion at an unknown later date.

But all this has a sense of tremendous busyness and activity, leaving us feeling we have accomplished things ! As we go along we make do with what we have and this makes major withdrawals from our energy and enthusiasm bank balances, till we resign ourselves to living with inconvenience and a poverty stricken future.

Bringing passion and purpose to performance allows us to create the right architecture and platform for our dreams to rise to celebrate a rich and rewarding present and a promising future.

The Third Lesson is "Blueprint your Life with Clear Purpose and Embed Your Soul in the Achiever's Hallowed Hall of Fame"

I : Integrity of Intent

Integrity is like a precious stone. A flaw in the stone will not only devalue the stone but also may cause problems for the wearer. Interestingly enough Integrity begins with "I" which means that it lies within us to manifest. The completeness or wholeness of the Purpose we bring to our performance and relationships as well as the truthfulness and honesty of our intentions, allow us to shed the disguises and garbs of "strategic" intent which is usually opportunistic in favour of an upstanding unconditional largeness of intent which enlarges the playing field to accommodate others too.

Amidst the fog of deviousness, manipulation and exploitation, integrity of intent is a clear beacon which illuminates the entire relationship with the purity of true partnership in progress.

The Fourth Lesson is "Be of Global Intent and Design. Leave Parched Parochialism to Wither and Die in the Sunshine of Abundance"

R : Reliability in Relationships

The word relationship itself shows us that just like a ship, all hands must be on the deck and the ship of relation needs the synergy of all members to pull together, especially in rough weather.

This applies to teams and associates at the organizational level or families and friends at the individual or personal level.

Navigating the storms and tempests of suspicion, doubt, misgivings, moments of weakness, inadequacies and incompetence, can take a severe toll on the most weather-beaten of sailors afloat on the sea of survival and success.

Establishing a resourceful relationship which counts on the contribution of all elements in the network of life, trusting and respecting those in the network and staying with the ship provides the robustness to the relationship. Investing in the relationship unconditionally by contributing first without calculating the returns, and living all the tenets we have described this far, creates the reliability needed to put wind in the sails.

It is all about being there when it matters. Finding the right role to play and a set of convergent goals to guide individual contributions to the relationship is crucial for one to deliver at least what is expected.

The Fifth Lesson is "Run a 24x7 Relationship with Your Resources. Burn Your Leave Card"

E: Excellence as a Way of Life

Making excellence a way of life, means demolishing the middle class of mediocrity and aspiring for the "dance of delight". Life at the cutting edge of excellence, cannot possibly be played by performing with competences one is conscious of possessing. Instead the thrill and exuberance of a full-blown life comes from reaching higher than the "essential expected" and delivering at the very "pinnacle of performance". It's all about asking yourself if what you do is enough or can you go the extra mile.

Pulling performances from the slums of mediocrity can be one of the most rewarding and thrilling experiences one can have. Like an eagle, once you experience the heavens, it is hard to live below the clouds. Finding refuge in being "grounded" or "down to earth" or "in touch with reality" leads to exactly that in the rewards. You are grounded in the earth, immersed in a false sense of security of a rationalized reality instead of soaring to embrace the universe.

The Sixth Lesson is "Live Life at Full Stretch Benchmarking Beyond the Best"

With these Six Lessons of Life may you fulfill your dreams and ASPIRE actively for all the success that the world can possibly offer.

WHAT'S IN STORE FOR YOU IN THIS BOOK

This book has several Success Scripts on various aspects of life Feel free to read from anywhere because each article has its very own precious nugget of wisdom

It is a compilation of such wisdom-pods which can appeal and relate to different people for different reasons. And to you too, at different points of your life.

Read and connect the wisdom they contain with the elements of your own life. That matters more

You must ultimately write your own success script. That's when you shall take charge of the wheel and steer the ship of your life to the wide-open seas of success

1
AT THE STEERING WHEEL OF LIFE
ENABLING YOUR LIFE TO DELIVER SUCCESS

Life is a mixed bag. What we package it with is what appears to the outside world as our lifestyle. Because that is what we wish to present to the world. Within the package however, is what it really is. If you do work on carefully constructing your life to a plan, or living as authentically as you can, you may find that not always is the packaging distinctly different from the contents of life. The best wrapping is a transparent one which reveals the contents for what it is and the blend it forms as one contrasting colour or layer from each life experience and learning, merges with another.

When we join our lives with another, as we do in marriage or at work in teams or professional partnerships, what we seek is a blend of lifestyles : of competences, of outlooks and approaches, where often one lifestyle leads another at different points of time, very much like rotating leadership. There are times when the blend is so good that it is hard to differentiate one from the other.

Yet the individuality of each lifestyle is what counts in differentiating key operational arenas to increase or maximize the probability of success.

Today we are faced with certain challenges and tomorrow perhaps with others. We have to look at each challenge separately and at how we handle them and which partner can handle it best. Once this is clear, then all that has to be done is to support the front line, in other words, actively support as one body , the person taking on the challenge directly.

Goals and Dreams

All of us have our own goals and ambitions, dreams and desires, methods and means by which we want to go about achieving them. Some of them are in sharp contrast to the other. However the common thread in all we do, has to embody, the essentials of life – which are – *a clear sense of self worth, courage of conviction, determination to succeed, honesty of approach, strength of purpose, responsibility for results and a sense of practicality* to guide and harness these to achieve our objectives.

Yes, it is important to manage all these qualities such that no single quality exists at the expense of the others. Especially true, where the sense of practicality often overpowers the rest and seeks relief in manipulating the means, to achieve a rationalized practical end.

It is also true that courage of conviction should not bestow a blindfold on reality.

Balancing Life's Imbalances

As you can see, this is a balancing act. The Scales of Libra if you may ! Equilibrium is achieved only after the balancing beam has tipped on either side.

Each side is you and somebody else- in your personal life it could be your spouse or your parents or your children or in your professional life it may be your boss or your team; and the balancing beam of the scale of our life is poised on the fulcrum of matured sensibility that holds us on even keel.

And to keep this even keel, each of us have to put in the correct measure of weights against values , means for ends, efforts for results, in each pan.

Values and Purpose

Values across life so far, for most of us, are attached to a very strong sense of purpose and strength of resolve to succeed against all odds. Many among us would have faced some of the worst nightmares, which have taken our entire reserve of courage in our convictions and determination to pursue our beliefs.

The task is to ensure that we do not abandon the struggle, but instead stare it in the face at frighteningly close quarters. We have had to ask ourselves very difficult questions and verify the "bonafides" of our own values. At the end, you would have found that the greatest comfort is in doing what you know is right even when this makes the terrain treacherous.

Winning with the Right Values

Winning is the right result, but, the means is very important too. And ever so often, you may find yourself at the non-preferred end of a rather discomforting duel to maintain Life's precious balance. In a world that rushes you through life like white-water rapids, the struggle is to first keep afloat and somehow manage to steer your war clear of the dangers that present themselves at each churning twist and turn. Life is in today's competitive world, an unsettling yet exciting experience ! The sheer thrill of being on board your own life is hard to be matched. Staying at the helm and steering your way through unchartered waters is a task that separates the strivers from the strugglers.

No successful ship laden with precious cargo is far from the radar of pirates ! Life has its share of buccaneers and pirates. Many successful lives have run aground for reasons ranging from being asleep at the wheel to the comforting swell of mediocrity in deep waters to arrogant navigation flying in the face of Life's tempests to mutiny to hostile takeovers. Of all these, the worst would probably be the handing over of your wheel mid-stream success, at the sharp end of a sword !

Defending your rights against those who want to snatch them away, calls for but one answer. Active defense, and not meek conciliation.

Especially when a sense of practicality tells us that we are capable of mounting not just a defense but an offensive. Negotiation is the route of least defense, when there is no other avenue open.

Happiness and success are NOT NEGOTIATED.

They are fought for. They are worked for. They are earned and then they are DEFENDED and PROTECTED with all one's might. This calls for an active engagement with one's life, not a casual enquiry. Investigate, Illuminate, Initiate, Innovate, Integrate your skills, competences, resources, align every thought and feeling and put every fiber and sinew of your body into

21

the task of retaining and rejoicing in your right to a vibrant life.

I do not sketch Life as one big battlefield, but it certainly is no rose garden.

The Big Question is : Are you WILLING to negotiate your happiness, your right to life, your future, your family, your marriage and your children and their future, with circumstance or worse, those who feed off the average man's hopes, dreams and aspirations.

Shall you SUCCUMB to a path of least resistance and offer your hard earned present and your well deserved future , on a platter to circumstance or those who have the effrontery to malign it ??

Would you BE JUDGED by circumstance or those who have no right to judge you and will you rather CLOAK YOUR COURAGE with the mantle of meekness ??

You must succeed as who you are and cannot succeed as who you are not. But first, you need to believe in **yourself** . And get a special someone else to believe in you. Happiness can be yours. Success shall fill your cup of life. Only when you are proud of who you are , what you have done, and to whom.

So here are Ten Tips and Tasks for a Productive Life :

1. Believe in Yourself – You Count !

    a.   List your Strengths

    b.   List successful Moments of Truth in your life

    c.   List Positive Feedback you have received

    d.   Write an Appreciative Letter to yourself

    e.   Write One Thing you do well that others don't or cannot do

2. Put Your Entire Energy into What You Do- It's Your Signature !

    a.   Make every moment special

    b.   Check what you have done for excellence

    c.   Set standards for yourself

    d.   Sell your work to yourself

    e.   Make a Masterpiece of any work you do.

3. **Value and Respect Others, No Matter Who They Are or What They Do – You Can Learn From Anyone !**

   a. List Your Everyday Advisors and their Key Advice

   b. Write a positive note on How to Use each Key Advice

   c. Make it important to Try each Key Advice and Record the Result

   d. Write down Who You Discount or Discredit as Capable of Sound Advice and Why

   e. Write down at least 2 Good Points about those you have put in the "Discredit List"

4. **Experiment and Experience Life – Move Out of Your Shell !**

   a. Describe a Typical Day in your Life

   b. Write what New Things you have done each day for the past Ten days

   c. Write down Things that you Want to do in Life but Do Not Dare to

d.   Write down Positive Outcomes and Negative outcomes for each

e.   Write down How you will Handle each Negative Outcome successfully

5. Learn to Forgive Yourself and Others – But Do Not Encourage Incompetence !

a.   Make a list of all the mistakes you can recall you have made in the past one year

b.   Put down reasons for each mistake and classify them into 3 categories – PERSONAL (identify whether Lack of Knowledge or Lack of Personal Competence / Skill / Ability), CIRCUMSTANTIAL (Due to Situations out of Your Control), or PROVOKED (because of Other People's interference/ incorrect advice / involvement)

c.   Write down consequences of each mistake

d.   Decide how you will handle each consequence to produce a Positive Outcome

e.   Examine each PERSONAL error and write down what you have to do to strengthen yourself in the areas of Knowledge, Skills and Capabilities to improve your overall Competence

6. **Keep an Open Mind, Learn to Coexist with Differences- In People and their Opinions and Views**

   a. Make a list of people you do not like – people known to you personally or professionally

   b. Write what you find wrong with each one of them

   c. Put down honestly, at least one clear bias or prejudice you hold against each one

   d. Examine the link between your bias or prejudice and your judgment about these people

   e. Write down honestly any small agreement you may have with each view or opinion you have rejected or discarded

7. **Take Charge of Your Life – Be Alert at the Wheel, Learn to Accelerate, Chart Your Course, Follow the Signs, Decide Your Breaks, Fill Your Tank and Turn On the Music too !**

a. Write down One Dozen things you are trying to accomplish at the moment

b. Write down your progress against each one – use a scale of 0 to 10 where 10 is the maximum accomplishment score

c. Put down what is blocking you against each of these one dozen items

d. As a consultant , recommend to yourself, what you should do to overcome these obstacles

e. Write down how you will celebrate each success in overturning each obstacle, and make sure you do it

8. Make Sure You Have Passengers in Your Car too- Carry Others along with you, Create Wealth for Others too !

a. Make a list of the closest people you live with and those you work with.

b. Write down for each one what you think are their needs and concerns

c. Write down what you do well and what capabilities you possess to do those things well.

d. Put down against each thing you do well, how you can help each one of the people you have listed earlier

e. Make a silent promise to each one you have listed that you will help them in someway, no matter how small.

9. **Be Humble Not Arrogant, but Market Yourself Vigourously and Honestly !**

a. Write down a complete list of all your possible strengths and capabilities

b. Create affinity clusters of these and write down the results they can help produce or deliver, regardless whether you currently have the opportunity or not.

c. Write down who needs to know about each of these strengths and capabilities.

d. Make an appointment with at least 3 key people from your list.

e. Discuss your strengths and capabilities with these 3 key people and ask them how and when they can use your talents.

10. **Keep revisiting Your Goals (roadmap) and Keep a Clear Eye on the Road too- Stay**

Focused on the Present while Working out the Future !

a.   Write a list of everything you could possibly want in life

b.   Qualify each one as Short Term, Medium Term and Long Term, using your own definition of the time frame for each

c.   Put deadlines for all Short term goals and list at least 10 immediate activities or tasks you need to perform to achieve them.

d.   Draw flexible time-lines for each Medium Term and Long Term goal and list at least 10 short term activities / tasks you must perform to achieve each one

e.   Raise red flag check points on all time framed activities and tasks

Decide **today** to take charge of your ship by being awake and alert …………..

At the Steering Wheel of Your Life !

2
LEADING ON THE EDGE
AT THE CUTTING EDGE OF COMPETENCE

Management gurus and their disciples, thinkers, strategists and business process re-engineers have been busy propelling the corporate world and the corporate mind into not only coping with, but also keeping in step with the rapid changes of an ever shrinking, increasingly competitive and exhaustingly demanding global market.

Undoubtedly the 21st Century is playing host to the greatest revolution in communication the world has ever seen, and consequently, the businesses of today will have to constantly re-engineer and restructure their approach, ever so keenly, to first survive and then ride the crest of this tidal wave of change.

Today, the ability to mass communicate instantly, has drilled right down to the level of any individual choosing to use the Net, and is no longer the sole domain of large corporate houses with inflated advertising budgets. Information and yes, dis-information can be broadcast for over a billion to view, in the mere blink of an eye. Business transactions on the Web, or e-commerce as we know it, is only part of the almost immeasurable progress the world has achieved in less than a decade, decidedly overshadowing the undeniably tremendous evolution of the world over the preceding half century.

The   Changing   Times   and   Tools
As times change, so have the tools of the trade. Today anybody in the business without a certain savvyness on the internet or for that matter without a personalized email address or a Home Page on the World Wide Web, may as well close shop and go home. A dinosaur.

From the beginning of time, as the world and life itself evolved, Mankind has constantly striven to push the pace of progress, leaving the weak to die, and the strong to live and thrive. We called it the process of Natural Selection. And as I reflect on the changing world, so it seems today too, with even greater ferocity and ruthlessness.

The arithmetic is very simple. The size of the pie being

constant, to eat more of it, somebody else has to go hungry. That is, unless somebody has the wisdom and the ability to make another pie and another. Business strategy is increasingly pointed in this direction. How to make another pie!

QUESTION 1 : Describe the Pie (your life or career or expertise or competence) you are feeding on at the moment and do you feel you have a privileged place at the table to get a good share of it ?

QUESTION 2 : If YOU had to make another Pie, because Pie # 1 will soon be devoured, what would that Pie be ? In other words, can you bring additional or new competences and opportunities to your career-table to increase your earnings or capacity to earn ?

Reconstructing the Ladder

For a business of the new millennium to succeed, organizational structure and operations have to be focused towards the Sun — that is, the entire organization and its various subsystems have to be energized to support each other, in one common direction. Organizational structure has to be redesigned or reconstructed to support operational efficiency and effectiveness. Knowledge based competences have to be ushered to positions of leadership.

Whether product or people, success will lie with those at the cutting edge of technology and a finger firmly on the market pulse. An explosive combination, such as this is, will always keep the business Leading on the Edge!

QUESTION 1 : What is your role in your organization ? How pivotal is it towards the success of the organization ?

QUESTION 2 : What is the life span of your current role ? What do you wish your role to be in the evolving organization? What efforts are you making to keep up with the market trends and shifts ?

The Kaizen of Learning

To arrive here, would necessarily involve continuous learning — structured training and exposure to the market needs, constant communication with the market place and the ability to discern, decide and function independently at critical operational levels of the organization, especially those interfacing with the market.

In the emerging market order, the factory will no longer produce what it simply can produce, of original capability or capacity, but will bend every resource it has or has to procure , to supply what the market demands of it — be this product or service. Because the customer (read you and me too !) now has literally, a world at his or her fingertips, and the decision making process has crashed down to almost a heartbeat.

Marketplaces have already begun to shed their parochial boundaries, and with the world increasingly becoming one giant market, any business, which seeks to dictate terms to the market, is perilously close to the edge of survival.

Protection to local industry has been slowly and painfully recognized as insulating them from the real world. Enhancing their growing incompetence in the false bliss of restricted competition, leaves them totally unprepared for the awaiting onslaught, when the curtain on competition is raised.

QUESTION 1 : What does the Kaisen of Learning mean personally to you ?

QUESTION 2 : What is your Personal Improvement Plan ? How and when shall you measure progress ?

The New Reality : Wake up or Die

Needless to say, horrible deaths await such placid and in the most liberal sense, merely "reactive" organizations. It would therefore be a matter of plain common sense that at the micro level, should you ever as an individual, feel protected and comfortable, this is to be feared most. Because this means, that you have already lost touch with reality.

It seems to me that , anybody within reach of reality, must always recognize the compelling need –of discomfort, of constant change, of threat to survival, of creating and fostering change, of continually learning, of challenging the established norm and only when you can catalyze change continuously, can you truly consider yourself to be Leading on the Edge.

The organization that must carry this task through will demand man-management skills of a dimension far superior than ever before. Even today, empowerment of manpower has become the watchword of progress in Human Resource Development efforts across the globe. Every man, must view the business as the CEO regardless of his position in the organization, says one management guru, for the view is best at the top.

QUESTION 1 : Are you a Caterpillar or a Butterfly ? How do you know ?

QUESTION 2 : What must you do to kill the Caterpillar in you, so that the Butterfly is set free ?

The Organizational Pyramid : shaken and stirred

In order to do this, unshackling the operating executive from the bonds of traditional organizations forms part of the key objectives of an enlightened management. It is a known fact that, any business entity is as good as the people who represent it. Tapping and cultivating individual potential has reached Critical Mass point in context of the business environment today.

The pyramidal Boss-Subordinate structure has to give way to flatter organizational structures, with teams of people spearheading identified tasks towards a larger common goal, interlinked with each other-, cross functionally too, providing a freer and wider berth of operation, with authority and responsibility extending beyond localized short term goals and targets, to encompass the overall aims and objectives of the organization.

The role of the traditional Boss, or the CEO of the firm – this may even be the Head of a Department or Division - has to mature into one of being a Facilitator and Motivator.

At the cutting edge of business competence, the strenuous demands on individual performance and achievement need to be complemented and supported with the Boss providing a highly positively charged work environment, along with the necessary tools of the trade, continuous training in the techniques to perform and produce results, counseling at regular intervals and most importantly, leading from the front.

QUESTION 1 : Today WFH or Working From Home has not only become necessary in the moment but seems sure to identify the future organization. What is your level of comfort with this new way of working ? Does it increase or decrease control over desired outcomes ?

QUESTION 2 : How well will you seek or use the skill of delegation to share power and control, increase accountability, flex independent competence and grow to greater levels up the organizational pyramid ? Personally and for your team if you have one.

Frontline Leadership

No better performance and achievement can be demanded, than by the sheer example of the leader. This has been one of the most major transformation in management thinking in recent times, and more often than not, organizational performance can be judged not just by that of the team, but more so, that of the team leader, Leading on the Edge, himself!

AT THE STEERING WHEEL OF LIFE

The new order of world business today demands performance right from the Top of the Pyramid, which provides the platform on which organizational vision , goals and targets to achieve this vision are laid in clear view of every element in the organizational network.

Skilled man-managers should easily recognize that High Performers and Achievers (HPA) have to be recognized and allowed to perform with the complete support of the system.

QUESTION 1 : Are you a HPA of your organization ? Are you visible to the organization leadership or are you working in the shadows ?

QUESTION 2 : What do you need to do to get into the line of vision of those who matter ? Do you have a plan you can sustain ?

The Power of Knowledge, the Might of Technology : Staying relevant to the business

Typically a high performer will also be high on knowledge and techniques of the trade, which have to be continually updated to keep abreast with the times. They will also often be subject to self-imposed high level stress, as a result of such high performers demanding more of themselves than even the organization does of them.

Their paranoia of complacency and stagnation, driven by a very high order of ambition, is the very force that powers the organization forward.

And they no longer need to fear for their jobs, for they are always in demand. They must have the freedom to choose the environment in which they can perform best, to their own lofty expectations of themselves. They exercise the choice to stay or go. And more often than not, they choose to go. Not always because they are dissatisfied , but because they have better options at each level of success.

QUESTION 1 : How are you dealing with your stress and stressors ? Do you feel you enjoy the engagement or are you feeling crushed ?

QUESTION 2 : What are your Core Drivers of Life ? How are they feeding your Ambition ? Do you have a plan to engage with these drivers in the role you perform or are you working actively on how these can take you to the next level ?

The Price of Success

The price usually paid by an organization on a victorious battle pitch, is the poaching of its top lieutenants. Organizations will have to recognize the inevitability of this and plan for it, with what is now being called the perpetuation of, or at least restricting the flight of, Intellectual Capital. In addition to the tangible ingredient "knowledge" which can be data based , intangibles form the other vital ingredients which cover Capital Resources involving the Company Management , the Employees, the Customer and indeed the Processes built into the system.

Almost any company on the Edge of Competitiveness and Growth would realize that their business is not just a result of well oiled systems working in unison, but instead, the cutting edge is indeed provided by the people who operate these systems. People involvement will always mean un-catalogued information and personalized knowledge, that affects the company and its business, often not shared with the system.

QUESTION 1 : If you lead a team, how prepared are you to sustain high performance and achievement if some members of your team leave or get poached ?

QUESTION 2 : If you decide to leave the organization, how much have you done to create a replacement who will step in and step up to the job ? Are you promoting growth in your team ? Personally, are you creating sufficient new critical competence, to be capable of bargaining or negotiating fresh terms to stay and grow in the same organization ?

The Twain shall Meet : the knowledge and information expressway to success

Managing the flow of information within the company and the smooth transfer of knowledge, where stagnant knowledge repositories are transformed into dynamic vehicles of growth, is one of the special skills that will daunt the abilities of corporate leaders.

While top human resources of a company can turn out to be, a critical casualty of success, in this New Millennium, more than ever before, any organization that can attract, nurture, retain, continually motivate and empower such people, and can at the very same time, conserve and build on its intellectual capital, will find itself invariably Leading On the Edge of Success.

3
EEK-ONOMICS
MAKE A U TURN IN THE DOWNTURN

Life promises to surprise. Just a while ago we were polishing our shining economy and patting the bloated belly of our envisaged future. Suddenly the winds of fortune turned out to be gas ! A case of the economy suffering from grave dyspepsia with the indigestible servings of the high and swinging life of over-indulgence. A few pills of stark reality put paid to the gas, and it passed with the awful sound and odour of production and job cuts.

So here we are back to our flat bellied world, only to find that we have purged more than necessary from the system. We have had to let go growth-steam , production- rhythm , momentum of change, motivation to experiment, learning ladders of progress, tenets of teamwork, enrolment of ethics, relationship realty, partnerships and scores of nutrients that are needed to fill the system with sustainable growth and competitive advantage. And all because the global pandemic of 2020 supplied the enema of deflated vision, and this along with powerful doses of survival laxatives impartially washed out all elements in the tubes !

Weakened at the knees of stability and glassy-eyed from the spasms of painful "detoxification" of the business blueprint of growth, one can be excused at despairing at the shrunken and emaciated remains of a thriving life. Blown away and blown apart are the lives of thousands and for countless generations onwards this effect will snowball to create of the greatest revolutions of economic life on the planet. What do we do with this sick world ? Well the best thing is to dig in your heels on the slopes of the downturn and force through a U- turn.

Lets look at what we can all do to chip in during these tough times. My guess is that it is very similar to what we do when we are really sick. We get a diagnosis done, medicate as advised, support the recovery process, stay in the groove keeping hope of recovery alive, get back up as soon as one can, allow recovery to complete the journey beyond the sensation of wellness, plant flags of our learning on the way ahead, learn new ways to be more resilient and forecast how to deal with future illnesses resident on the journey and thus achieve a new fullness of health which promises to be more resilient and immune to the bacteria of breakdown.

Translate this to the times of today, and we can look beyond the "medication" which is in progress, and work out the steps from supporting recovery to future new health. The organization and the individual can work in tandem to produce the armour we require.

Lets see what the Individual (you) can do for himself (yourself) :

- **Use the time available to get back into shape** – health, knowledge, skills and abilities.

- **Enroll your hobbies** into your mainstream of life – the future may lie there instead.

- **Recast your lifestyle** – critically examine what you need and what are the excesses that can be cut away.

- **Repair, Reframe and Renew the life you have** – revisit old practices like walking instead of driving , visiting instead of emailing , using cost effective public systems in transport and communication instead of costly private luxuries , budget-shops instead of glitzy malls with expensive distractions, more meals at home instead of fast food take aways and glamorous dining at starred restaurants, a quiet and enjoyable sip of wine at home with the family at dinner, rather than the wallet shaking pub crawling crave, living with the fashion statements already in your closet rather than the ones in magazines and showroom windows, more polish on the shoe leather instead of new leather- old leather is so much more comfortable, and well... you complete this list !

- **Invest in the future rather than spend for the present, because the future is still available.** So educate yourself further with well chosen courses that add value to your future, certify your knowledge and pick up additional skills by examining what your natural talents and abilities can do for you if cultured them beyond passing interest to professional undertaking.

- **Provide yourself with options by creating them from the "meta-markets" of your life-skills**. For example, if you are a good teacher, learn to become a professional life-coach, a trainer, a counselor. Or if you sing well, train your voice professionally, if you are knowledgeable and skilled, learn to teach and pass on the baton of success to others, if you like gardening , learn to landscape, if you draw and paint, then start offering your skills to printing and publishing houses, learn and certify yourself in computer animation courses, if you like cars and bikes, learn how to repair them, learn how to design them, if you like playing with colour, learn how to apply it in industrial design and interior decoration and so on.

- **Combine incomes, skills and lives**- get back to community living. Try the new-old way of sharing with family or creating sharing families with friends. Let your networking skills create synergistic skill and life networks that live the practice. It will help you build organizations for the future. You may never need to "get-back-to-work" !

What can the organization do to help in these challenging times ?

Well to begin with the organization jumbo-jet can pull full throttle on the twin-engines of good governance and corporate social responsibility. These are those very engines of growth they have touted and won awards for in the "good-times" and must now fly in their passengers (read employees , channel partners, vendors and stakeholders etc) in the "bad-times" . Because the passengers are on board since they have already bought their tickets which paid for the fuel and carriage , and cannot be simply jettisoned because the pilot and crew

are incompetent to perform to full emergency measures
!

This would call for measures such as :

- **Counseling the employees** what to expect of the future in this business

- **Increasing the level of in-house expertise** through training and development activities in a focused manner to support and sharpen skills directly related to business

- **Stepping up motivation** by involving close examination of the hygiene and motivational factors and what strengthening of these would result in better performances.

- **Conducting talent identification processes** to identify what talents other than those aligned to business are available and counseling employees how they can use their talents to cope with the future.

- **Creating creative "brain-shops"** in the organization to examine extreme and diverse ways of leapfrogging or re-scaling or reframing and reinventing business life cycles.

- **Cutting the flab from business spend** across the organization rather than simply cutting salaries and jobs.

- **Investing more in focused operations** like R&D and product distribution rather than advertising and promotional gimmickry.

- **Moving from cost-cutting to cost-reduction** as a design not a mere measure.

Together the twin clasp of individual and organizational effort to stem the hemorrhaging flow of talent, competence, capability and opportunity can help restore some of the equilibrium to the violent see-sawing of life today.

None of the suggestions offered are all consuming or exhaustive, not do they prescribe fortune filled futures, but they do allow you to dig in your heels and gouge the hell out of the downslide to slow you down enough to craft the U-turn after which the real hard work begins-going back up the hill !

KEY QUESTIONS :

- What is it that you have in mind for yourself ?
- What can you do for your team ?
- What can you do to create new opportunities for growth ?
- How dependent are you on others in the organization to do this ? Can you change this ?

4

THE SCRIPT OF LEADERSHIP

IGNITING AN INSPIRING WAY OF LIFE

Adapted from the book

The Butterfly Blueprint by Dexter J Valles

Are you a Great Leader ?

I wonder what your answer is, to this seemingly simple question. I hope of-course that you answered in the affirmative. However if you didn't, maybe you should reconsider what you need to do to be a leader.

Quite often many consider leadership to be a designation in an organizational hierarchy. It is certainly so. And much more than that. It goes beyond designation. Because designation defines a role and details what you need to do.

While to be a Leader, you need to BE a Leader ! The landscape is much larger. A manager manages tasks and can also lead. A leader always leads. At times, from behind. That's because Leadership is an inspiring and influential way of life.

Leadership is about leading, inspiring, influencing and launching people to the Vision and Purpose of the organization or community.

Lets look at what comprise the characteristics of Leadership

I like to call them the *6 Cs of Leadership*

Competence

To be counted on for your knowledge and expertise in the area you lead. Its not necessarily technical skill but certainly a high level of mastery of and immersion with the subject or market or industry.

A competent leader says " I've got this "

Courage

Stand up for your values and beliefs. Stand up for your people

Have courage of your convictions. Draw the line and stand firmly yet not obstinately. Have the courage to admit your mistakes and to apologize.

A courageous leader says " You have me in your corner"

Compassion

It is good to be tough and strong willed. Good to be determined and powerful. In all that, remember to be just and kind. Learn to lift people up not beat them down. Forgive others. Forgive yourself. Practice living with abundance and gratitude.

A compassionate leader says " I understand you"

Conscience

It's your lighthouse which must always illuminate the way in the darkest of nights. Your sense of right and wrong, just and unjust, fair and unfair, context and content. Your inner voice always rings your truths. Learn to listen.

A conscientious leader says " You can count on me to do what's right"

Coherence

Let your heart, mind and soul operate with clarity and coherence with what you do. Because that is who you are. No matter how or when or where you are observed or experienced, the stories told of you, must fall in place to form the picture of the world you strive to create.

A coherent leader says " All of me is fully and completely here and clear on how I can lead you with clarity to our shared vision"

Consistency

One of the hallmarks of leadership is the consistency with which you demonstrate your leadership. The regularity and reliability of your performance, your engagement with the business, the people, the message you endorse, the vision you describe. People look for leaders they can count on to walk their talk, every time they experience them.

A consistent leader says " You will always find me here"

The **7th C** (Bonus) is **Coachability**.

A leader must be willing to continually learn. A learning leader builds a learning organization or a community of learners. A leader must be open to feedback, to reflect on them and reach for support from others. To be coachable is to be aware of ones own shortcomings, the gaps between promise and performance in the pursuit of fulfilling purpose, to be humble to seek and engage support and guidance, yet determined to own the journey.

A coachable leader says " I too must learn with you to rise up. Push out my limiting boundaries. To be more competent, courageous, compassionate, conscientious, coherent and consistent"

So what does a leader need to DO in order to BE a leader worth following ?

I believe every Leader needs to embrace an agenda of Everyday Leadership

An agenda of everyday engagement. In order to embody the ability to influence and inspire people. As a way of living the truths they proclaim.

Listen & Learn

The truth is in common sight outside. Pay close attention to what the returning message is saying. Is it close to the message you sent out ? What came back ?

Engage Emotions (Hearts not just Hands)

People must feel valued and appreciated. Either that or they feel neglected. Hardly anyone can claim effectiveness and agility in performance when the heart is heavy. Neutrality is a myth. Emotions influence if not direct our actions. Emotions when engaged positively radiate into the environment connecting others to the vision.

Activate & Accelerate

Be the spark and the flame. Let knowledge and skill combine to create new standards of performance. Create competence and capacity. Build a groundswell of good practices and processes which will lift people to the performances they desire to deliver.

Develop (others) & Delegate

Holding on to power or position does not define true leadership. Real leaders give away powers, making others powerful too. Leaders don't create followers. Leaders create more leaders. The King maker versus the King.

There is enough powerful positive available in the world to lift every single human being to their potential. Delegating wisely, and not dumping, help people develop and grow into their power. A powerful organization is a community of powerful positively engaged people performing to their potential.

Enlarge the Ecosystem

As a leader we influence the ecosystem we operate in. We can either size it down and make it small, narrow, compartmentalized and confined so its easily manageable. Or we can choose to increase the challenge by opening the canvass to full spread. Reorient roles to break down the barriers of mindsets, of parochial performances, of filtered vision, glass ceilings and partitions. Encourage the spirit of entrepreneurship. Lead people to the ocean, not wade in streams.

Redirect & Reshape

Create a pulsating organization. Be constantly aware of the journey and willing to redraw the map, redirect energies and reshape outcomes to serve the common vision of a dynamic metamorphic organization in step with a constantly evolving living planet.

So in conclusion, in the context of creating leaders worth following, it needs leadership character to be forged in the cauldron of an everyday way of life. It would demand that every leader must Learn while Leading, Engage Emotions of the people, Act Decisively with the 6Cs , Develop People's Potential not just performance, Evolve Personally by pushing limiting boundaries and embrace Risk by learning to play outside the boundaries of Fear.

A Leader must leave forward a Legacy. One that inspires others. To continuously strive to create a worthy world.

KEY ACTIONS :

Make a Blueprint for yourself to be a Great Leader (no matter who you are or what role you perform currently) based on whatever you have read from this article.

AT THE STEERING WHEEL OF LIFE

Connect with your actual life to detail what you wish to stitch into the design for Great Leadership

Write the LEGACY you wish to leave and let your Leadership Blueprint deliver it

5
POWERFUL LIVING
MAKING LIFE DELIVER DELIGHT

A delightful Sunday morning, around a dozen years ago in 2008, caught me uncoiling lazily in my bed, stretching the sleep out of my body and squinting against the sunshine streaming on the pillow. Choices had to be made- should I leave the safe zone of my comfortable quilts or uncover myself to the sunny reality slowly invading all corners of my bedroom ? Snuggling down deeper into the soft eiderdown I chose not to choose and decided to let my stresses of the week drain away slowly, until I heard my conscience calling loud and clear.

My conscience ? What was that ? Years after being a corporate citizen in an overly competitive world, I thought I had rid myself of it a long time ago ! My nearly four year old daughter it was indeed, standing firmly in its place instead, tugging at my eyelids and admonishing me in the most mature parent like voice she could manage " Come On Daddy, why are your sleeping ? It's a beautiful day outside ! "

Let An Angel Visit Your !

One of the great joys of being a father to a daughter is to be greeted by an angel in the morning and I reached out with both arms pulling her down and buried my face in her tummy making her squeal with delight and propping her upon my knees, enquired "So what does my sweetheart want to do today ?" That did it. The litany commenced " I want to go out, I want to ride in a bus, I want to go in that plane, I want to go to the beach, I want to go to Goa, I want to go shopping, I want to go and play, I want to go to my friend's house, I want to go to dance-school, I want to see that movie..." And she meant them all ! So began a day that as it progressed promised to burst at the seams, remarkably with more vigour and fun ending in an energy high that almost could not be run down !

Amazed aren't you ? Well so was I, but I recalled my own youth and how much we did and lived in one day, each day at a time. Powerful lives lived at full stretch. The cup really did run over.

So why do we live within the cup of our lives, why not let it run over any more. We seem to be happy with living contained lives, within the sanctuary of safety, responsibilities, focus, rationality, reasonableness, moderation and therefore Mediocrity !

Making Much of Mediocrity

Perhaps without realizing it, we have slid down the greasy pole of achievement and success to a level of happy mediocrity where life seems to be assured and the peril of striving to stay at the top is swapped with the comforting lull of "consolidation".

Something like hanging up the wanderer's backpack and parking your high-roads bike, for a log-house in a meadow and a stately sedan to carry the growing midriff of a "settled" life.

Seems interesting and the right thing to do at first, until you realize what you give up. We give up the spirit to explore our world, to savour the thrill that risk brings, the ability to live with less and still feel like a king, to give freely from what we have because there's nothing to miss when its gone; to delight with the discoveries of new avenues of living, the experience of experimenting.

We surrender the somewhat savage need to conquer, the untamed cry of the rebel against institutionalizing and corralling an exuberant life into straight-jacketed mellowness.

Dream to Dare

No longer daring to dream but merely dreaming to dare, no longer at the cutting edge of a razor sharp life, but on the blunted butt of "boringly balanced" sensibility.

After nearly three decades of driving a car with the four wheels of balance, I decided to buy myself a bike once again. An Enfield 350cc Thunderbird.

Why ? Because I needed to feel the wind whip my hair again, the rain splatter against my face, to bend and twist my thickened torso once again as I weave in and out of traffic, around sharp curves and the thrill of the balance between machine and man!

And the sheer joy of straddling the roar and throb of the powerful engine, a fantasy of machismo. Pure adrenaline indeed ! Brief moments of it are enough to energize my day beyond belief.

The ageing adult reliving the fantasies of an adolescent , one may say, but that was when all the undiluted fun and the raw power of life lay !

Balancing Opposites

Mating the maturity and assuredness of the sober adult with the reckless and fiery spirit of the unfettered child can be one of the most rejuvenating experiences in living life powerfully again.

Because this time around we have more options and are more capable of unlocking sensitive doors skillfully rather than battering them down with the brute force of unbridled and brash youth.

We can love without letting lust intervene, live with some risk rather than risk life, learn to unlearn and relearn instead of learning by rote, plan and do. Rather than "plan to do" or only "do and undo", acquire and give away. Rather than snatch and hide.

Succeed and support instead of fail and flail , aspire and acknowledge achievement rather than compete and crush the competition. Conquer and democratize rather than capture and dictate. Build shining towers of shared success rather than colonies of mediocrity.

Powerful living is not a dream. It is an aspiration in action.

Inscribe your own shining life-epitaph by crossing every point on the bucket-list you write with the blood of buoyant youth, the will of the achieving adult and the wisdom of the old.

KEY QUESTIONS :

Can you make life count once again and make a difference in the way you steer the wheel to make life deliver delight ?

What's the ZING you need to put into your life to feel truly alive ?

6
WHITHER THE QUALITY OF LIFE
MANAGING THE SEE-SAW OF WORK-LIFE BALANCE

How's Life ? All of us have been posed this question, at some time in our lives, if not almost every day by everyone we meet. And we usually shrug off the question with flippant dismissal. Very few of us are ecstatic or gush about how swell life is. Many of us reply with a weary sigh while some of us grimace with ill concealed pain. What we are really describing of-course is not life as in being alive and breathing, but instead, the Quality of Life we live.

I have often asked myself, what is the quality of life we seek, and could not help comparing life, to food, which is the easiest way to see whether we have or do not have, the recipe to make life tick. But lets talk about that later.

Childhood, the Cradle of Happiness; Seize every moment !

Among the majority of us fortunates, childhood is when life is most enjoyable, as bereft of responsibility, all we have to do is savour every wonderful moment in time, to the fullest. We are taken care of, sheltered, fed, clothed, educated and kept in good health. Whenever we take ill, all we have to do is lie back and recover. Nothing clutters the brain beyond the events of the day. It is often said that a child is happiest because he or she lives in the present with both mind and body as one unit.

On our journey through life we begin transferring the state of mind to the past and the future, in opposition to the body, thus causing what is commonly called Stress.

As young adults, life begins to bloom, as the mind and body are nourished with knowledge and metabolism, peaking to produce perhaps the finest co-ordination between the mental and physical states. Life is one great colourful flourish on the canvass of time. But what happens thereafter ?

The Perilous Path of maturity and focus
Youth moves on to maturity and we begin to gain "focus" on our lives and what direction we wish our lives to take.

Ambitions and achievements take the place of adventure.

Dedication and devotion to purpose replaces dare devilry. Deliberate professionalism prevails over impulsive intuition, while Career quests overshadow the carefree spirit, forging character and mettle of leaders and entrepreneurs .

Coping with stress, chaos, work-life imbalances, pressures of the daily grind, people relationships, demanding targets, conflicting goals, aspirations and professional paradigms of an ever changing world can be not only a daunting and challenging task but also a mentally and physically sapping ordeal !

And the Quality of Life ?

Executive stress, burnout , suicide, divorce are some of the answers, unless life resembles a balanced meal. Aha ! you say, and how is that so ? Well, consider this . Sometimes we assume life to be , only that part which takes up most of our time.

For the career chasers it is their vertical growth rate in the organisation or in their own business and for the homemaker , it is housework. All this reflects Quantity and not Quality. But not so with food !

The Quantity of Life ?

Almost anybody I know has dined out at a restaurant . When choosing where to eat , we invariably look for , not just good cuisine , but also the location of the restaurant, the parking service, the air conditioning, the music, the décor, the ambience , the nature of its current clientele and so on.. While all we really do is eat there. But the packaging and the surrounding benefits are so necessary and all so important to us. If so, then why do we judge life by just the food, or sometimes by just the main course ?

Why not package life such that even the most miserable meal or career glows in the ambience of the surrounding hobbies or career off-shoots?

Whenever I've sat down to order a meal , I invariably look for the accompaniments, and often enough, it is these that decide the success of the meal. I cannot get into my steak , no matter how delicious it looks, without my baked potatoes, spinach and boiled veggies and that pat of golden butter oozing goodness. I know of a fellow who went berserk when he did not receive his pickles with the food. It simply shows that not always is the quality of food or for that matter, life, defined by just the main serving , but often enough, it is the tiny add-ons that really decide the lip smacking goodness of life.

Packaging the Zing !

What are these add-ons that put the zing into life ? This is for each one of us to determine and can often be an absorbing hobby or sport or music or any parallel line of activity that brings in tangible fulfillment. Sometimes physical evidence of effort ploughed in, does not reflect as much as we desire, in our basic square meal in life. So we choose to bring in activities of our own , which meet this need.

I often offset my reverses or lack of results at work by creating my own successes, unto myself, if not to anybody else, through penning my thoughts and experiences into tangible form , either in prose or poetry. Energizing yourself becomes necessary to sustain the quality of living in the main life zones, usually career and family life. Somehow , if we were as fussy about the add-ons to our lives as we are in choosing the toppings for our pizza, life could become one big delight.

Life is a choice, like it or love it

Not all of us are fortunate enough to choose a line of work or career that dovetails comfortably with our skills or education or choice. Ideally , this is what we need to do, but haven't we often been told at the restaurant, that the very item we wished to savour, is not on the menu of the day ? So do we leave the restaurant and seek another one where we find what we want, even if it takes all night ? The chances are , we don't , and instead settle for next best ,or whatever else is available.

To reconcile to the misfiring of our carefully constructed plans, we can either open our minds to the new experience of what gets served in our plate, or disguise what we have with a whole lot of sauces and condiments , hoping to reconstruct something totally new , although with insufficient means to do so. Isn't life often frighteningly like that?

When we approach the Quality of Life, we more often than not, consider the Quantity of Life as the Quality of Life , and here is where we source our judgements on what our lives are all about. If we could only pause to listen to the winds of fresh thought whispering through our minds, we would certainly have cause for celebrating the true Quality of Life !

KEY QUESTIONS :

- What can you do to improve the QUALITY of your life ?
- What is blocking your way to this ? What do you need to do to move these blocks aside ?

7
BUS DRIVING
MY EMOTIONAL
ACCOUNT
MANAGING UNCONDITIONAL
POSITIVE RELATIONSHIPS

Sometimes in life you do things you do not understand and yet they deliver positive results. At a shallow level of analysis, the reasons underlying this can usually be found in some commonplace answers, everyday rules, basic values and perhaps a way of life that has been adopted not by choice but by old habit.

Sometimes later in life you may realize the profound lesson behind some of these events and the immense learning it can deliver to you on your difficult yet determined way to success.

Let me share a personal experience with you that follows these lines.

Many years ago, when I was a child, I experienced a strange relationship which I did not give much thought to, but now I see it for what it was and ever since I have realized the lesson it delivered , it has changed my life.

Our Family

I am the eldest of two children in a small family in Mumbai INDIA, where the family consisted my parents and also my ailing grandmother, my father's mother, his dad having passed on many years before. It also included an aging unmarried uncle, Dad's eldest brother, who though a hardy veteran of life in all its forms, had experienced terrible setbacks and had retreated to the safety of the family, a shelter from an unfriendly and hostile world.

My Father

My father was a quiet, industrious man with a strong sense of purpose and values. His humour was infectious and he embodied the "man of the house" status as if it were natural to him to deal with all the world had to shove at us, with the greatest equanimity I have experienced. Grandma's ailments kept taking a turn for the worse, and the world too seemed to have turned a shade darker. Yet my father went about what he had to do with more vigour and yet always found the time for us children to play, teach and live in pace with our growing worlds.

My Mother

My mother, was the perfect backbone the family needed. Talented and skilled in art, she set aside her career to look after grandma, and this lasted a long and arduous fifteen years. She was the rock in the family, on which dad could build the home. She was full of life, always busy, always loving, caring to the core, and for us kids, a safe haven to run to in times of trouble. In her arms, and they were strong yet immensely comforting arms affording incredible security, we could find great sanctuary from any form of danger. Mother was invincible.

She was later to hold the family together with my father through such terrifying times, that this invincibility was often battered, but never gave way.

Our invincible mother died early at the age of just sixty, six months after she helped my father recover from an unexpected heart attack on the eve of Christmas 2002.

Life Lessons

Through both parents we learned several life lessons, not the least being how to hold a family and faith together in violent turbulence. The smaller lessons are what this note is all about.

Helping around the house, running chores, growing up from levels of dependence to almost arrogant levels of independence can often scar behavior beyond recognition. But ingrained in us was the need to be decent and respect ourselves and others in all we did.

Role Model Parents

Dad was the role model here, his colleagues often telling us how much he stood apart from the others because of these traits. Mother followed up with the lessons we needed to learn to be like Dad. Respect everyone, she said, even those you feel are below your status, like the maid servant at home, the ordinary worker on the road, the shopkeeper attendant, the bus driver and bus conductor, the peon, other children, especially the deprived. Their pain and suffering were their badge of honour, she would say, their qualification for the right to an equal life.

Everyday Goodness

All this translated to simple greetings like " Good morning, Good afternoon, Good evening, Good night" and the all essential "Thank You" and " I'm sorry" It also meant never taking credit for anything that was not due or belonged to someone else, returning money or fulfilling payments immediately without waiting for even the next day to pass, paying our fair share, and being responsible and accountable for the little things we took charge of in and around the house.

The Project

We schooled quite a distance from where we lived in Mumbai's northern suburbs, about 15 km away, and with traffic and transport frequency being what it was around 45 years ago, mother took on the task of ferrying us back and forth, the school not having a regular bus service of its own. Poor experiences with a neighbouring school's bus which left us stranded in a monsoon flood in waist deep water left her so furious, she decided that her responsibilities must include this very difficult ordeal. So she made three trips per day, the one in between to bring us lunch, and yet managed a home almost entirely dependent on her to run. Even as carefree children and happy to see mother as often as possible, a beacon of warmth and safety, in the unfriendly environs a school often chooses to offer children; we could see the great strain this was on her. Yet she never complained.

To regulate life somewhat, mother chose a bus route that took us directly to school without any changeover midway. This meant being exactly in time for the bus and this being a ring route, we also caught the very same bus on the way back home. And so we became familiar faces being regular passengers on a generous part of the route itself. Mother as usual would prompt us to greet the conductor as we boarded the bus and thank the driver as we disembarked. We would then wave to the bus driver and conductor as the bus eased away from the bus stop.

People in the Place of Parents

The bus conductor was almost priestly in his disposition and demeanour. Silver haired and dignified, he would return our greeting with his own blessing for the day or the rest of it, while the driver, a burly sunburned toughie with a walrus like moustache , would break into the most delightful smile as we thanked him in chorus and later waved him goodbye.

And so life went on, for a couple of years, before I finally mustered the courage to assure mother that I could take care of my younger brother and steer ourselves and back form school safely, given the regimen we had established. Skeptical of success, but now terribly overburdened, mother made a few dry runs with us to check our navigational and other competences. She also asked the bus conductor and driver duo to "keep an eye" on us. A request they quickly agreed to comply with. But could you really expect a busy public transport employee, harassed by his very work, barely managing to keep his own equilibrium on even keel, to keep this promise ? Well, we were in for a surprise.

Like clockwork we managed to make the daily circuit without any incident worth mentioning or remembering. Life was settling down to an even regularity, as far as transport was concerned. Till one day this took a big jolt.

The Test

The school principal decided to lecture the school , for ten long minutes on some moral values of life after the evening prayer at the end of day. This meant that our timetabled life was now going to be turned on it's head.

The bus stop was a brisk 12 minute walk from the school door through the playfield, out of the gate, across the road at a busy traffic junction and then a straight run. This gave us 3 minutes to catch our breath and jostle in line to be the first to spring into the bus, my brother in front of me, held and shielded from the rushing crowd.

Once in, the usual greeting to the conductor and a run for empty seats if any or a position in the front so one could pick up casual conversation with the walrus-mustachioed driver.

Scrambling for freedom, the school exploded onto the road at the traffic junction just across the gate. Amidst the melee, stood a red bus, unmindful of the green signal to go, and the jarring honking of the traffic behind, pumping it's own loud horn in an SOS manner.

Puzzled, I looked up, and saw a great big burly face decorated with a walrus mustache, followed by half the burly body, leaning right through the driver's window calling us to board the bus. Grabbing my brother by the hand,

I raced across and boarded from the front, to be greeted with a loud cheer from the passengers, and a huge grin from the driver and a visibly relieved conductor. Thanking him profusely, we spent the remaining journey, being grateful for not being pushed into an unfamiliar route home or being delayed to a degree of discomfort.

Reflecting on the Lesson

The memory soon passed, until it rang several bells when I read Stephen Covey's thoughts about Emotional Bank Accounting. This concept is so simple and so real. It simply states that just like a financial bank, we deposit and borrow from people we deal with everyday. The account we use if the one we open with each and everyone we meet and work with.

It's called an Emotional Bank Account. Simply put, we need to have a minimum deposit and keep filling in the account to make it work. It helps when we have to make withdrawals.

The deposits are simple ones, like acknowledging the other, common courtesies, keeping the small promises we make, being sincere in helping, being sincere in owning up to mistakes made and apologizing with intent to repair the damage done and so on. The small stuff. But all this has to be made unconditionally without plans for withdrawals. No strings attached.

When withdrawals occur, like shortness of temper, demands on time and work priorities, abruptness with courtesies, anger mismanaged, and all the roughshod treatment we dish out liberally in a day, the unconditional deposits we have banked allow us to save the relationship from destruction.

So where does this leave my bus driver , all those many years ago ? You got it, the Emotional Bank Accounts we opened with them were liberally filled with the unconditional deposits of children not yet coached with the skills of opportunism of the world. Simple greetings from the heart of innocent children, filled the heart of these veteran workers of the daily grueling grind of life, to extend themselves to assume the role of parents , and reach out beyond call to fulfill this withdrawal they not just sanctioned but offered.

Emotionally Driven with A Promise of Protection

Keeping an eye on the clock, this grizzled bear of a driver, realized we would not make it on time, so he did the unthinkable, only a parent would do. Scanning the uniformed crowd of children, to search and find , two children from amongst hundreds, and get them on board, to keep a promise made so casually must have been the consequence of the EBA being driven right home.

KEY QUESTIONS

- Can you recall incidents from your life which sowed the seeds of empathy and emotional deposits ?
- How many relationships do you feel are crucial to your success at work ? Can you list them ?
- On a Relationship Success Scale of -100 to +100 can you identify the score of each of these relationships ?
- What can you do about relationships where the scores are low ?
- What about your relationship scores at home ?
- How are you going to make people fee they matter to you ?

8
LEADING & ENGAGING EMOTIONAL ENERGY
THE HEART OF EQ

Most of us are frontline citizens of the world in the most competitive times of our lives – the 21st Century, Year 2020 !! The Year of Transformative Change !

In these unprecedented demanding, high stress, high expectations and highly unpredictable times, we have to do everything possible to stay afloat, survive and thrive

Leadership in Transformed Business more than ever before needs to be a beacon in the New Ways of a New Volatile Uncertain Unpredictable and Complex Life !

AT THE STEERING WHEEL OF LIFE

Very often the complexity of the times we now live in, is a major challenge to how we feel, think and act. The stressors, the pressures, the demands of everyday life in this new context of the pandemic and locked down life emerging into the bright light beyond 2020, shall suck out our reserves of emotional energy. At the end of the day we are undoubtedly going to feel completely exhausted, unable to recover our energies in order to lead a productive, positive and powerful life.

Building Effective Business Relationships to Drive Results , especially in this emergent world beyond 2020 shall need us harness our Emotional Energy in a Powerful and Positive Way.

Where Energy Flows, so does Focus, and vice versa. When we allow the difficulties and differences of our relationships to overwhelm our energy and focus, we drive our decisions through that gauntlet. Often accompanied with ego clashes, errant values and power struggles.

Trust is a major casualty in the process. Relationships are torn apart with conflict. Conflict which perhaps began in the lockdown of our lives.

Business and Life itself can barely survive this. Once short-term commitments are seen through, entire relationships crumble. Partnerships transit into sullen silence. Or even more unfortunately, into active acrimony. Hardly the way to direct the energy of the people, teams and organizations beyond 2020

So where does it all go wrong ?

The questions we need to ask ourselves are:

Is our Heart (Emotional Balance) truly engaged with our Head (Wisdom & Knowledge) and Hands (Capability & Skills) ?

Do we really KNOW what is working and what is broken and needs fixing in our own behaviour and performance?

Can we CHOOSE to ACT with all three- Knowledge, Skill and Emotion ?

Are we ready to *seek help* to REFRAME & REINVENT our Leadership practices everyday in order to be more powerful, more capable and more successful ?

What will we GIVE of OURSELVES to gain this ? Will we be Influential Business Leaders whom others wish to engage as their Business partners ?

What's the Impact of Emotionally Intelligent Business Leaders and Managers

People with consistently high performance scores also have the most resilient EQ. In other words this shows a strong relationship between EQ competence and achievement

AT THE STEERING WHEEL OF LIFE

You may be surprised that it has been found that EQ contributes to

o Personal and social competencies that support growth of people and the organization

o Professional Approach and Attitude to Business Development

o Business Instinct – a combination of real cognitive competence, strategic purpose, clarity of vision, emotional engagement and gut instinct

o Accessibility, Accountability and Authenticity

o Engagement with Values and Core Principles that define and drive the Vision

o Empowerment of people to perform willingly and consistently at their very best.

o Work relationships and networking, inside and outside the organization

EQ is a way of looking "inside the engine" or "below the tip of the iceberg" at liberating the human being to search, find, acknowledge, accept and befriend the deepest darkest emotion within oneself. Because it is part of who you are.

As new world leaders, at conscious and unconscious levels, EQ competencies are constantly in flow. Engaging the EQ energy to electrify your emotional circuits effectively requires conscious attention and practice to make choices that question the trigger responses of your habituated behaviour. To suit the needs of a world beyond 2020 framed in the context of the Crisis of 2020

Regardless of the roles you represent at work or in your personal life, how you show up matters.

Whether you are a leader from Marketing or Sales or Customer Service or Finance or Legal or HR or Operations, you are wired to the business of your organization. And every transaction you make inside impacts the quality of the business delivered outside.

Here is your LEADERSHIP SIX PACK for the Road to High Impact Leadership with the Power of EQ

Meet Yourself to Know Yourself

Emotions play a significant role in your life. They direct your focus and attention to the issues you face and depending on how you manage your emotions , you make effective or ineffective decisions which impact your life and those of others too. It is therefore important to understand the seat of your emotions - the neuroplastic brain, which transforms with every thought you process.

The Emotional brain is where you can manage and coach your emotions to be more effective, but you need to be emotionally literate - to recognize, label and understand your emotions and the information they contain. When you can "meet yourself" we can get to "know yourself". This is the very first step towards developing emotional intelligence.

Understand Yourself - Measure Your Strengths & Competencies

Emotional Intelligence is often thought of as a description of your capability to manage your emotions effectively. However, Emotional Quotient or EQ is a measurement of how emotionally savvy you are. This is measured across emotional competencies which indicate what is being measured too. It is important that you work toward developing a wholesome development of emotional competence across all the EQ competencies.

EQ Competencies are most easily understood through the famed Six Seconds' EQ Competencies Model often called the KCG Model of EQ, Where it comprises 3 Key Pursuits: Know Yourself (Awareness of the range of Emotions you experience and Your Patterns of Behaviour) , Choose Yourself (Intentionality and the ability to pause, think about consequences and make better choices while remaining optimistic and motivated) and Give Yourself (Finding Purpose through Contributing with Empathy to the world, what you wish to receive from it. In short, building the world you want to live in)

Understanding the imbalances and shortcomings in your emotional competence make-up can give you great insight why you fall into emotional traps and why you make some decisions you are likely to regret later.

Your areas of strength in your bag of emotional competencies can help you develop your overall EQ savvy-ness by leveraging these strengths of your emotional character.

Learn to Navigate Life : Patterns Predict Possibilities.

Life is often like a choppy and churning sea hurling waves against the rocks or like a foaming whitewater river rushing over the edge into the chasm. We are all in that emotional-water, learning as we go, how to manage the swirl, heave and pulls of the raging currents of our emotions.

Navigating through your emotions to make the best sense of your life, needs you to have a blueprint of yourself, a kind of mind map of your emotional patterns, habits and compulsions.

You can then chart your course through these waters to the safety of your desired destination and achieve the results you seek. Otherwise you risk battering yourself against the rocks of your hijacked emotions or drowning in the churn of an emotionally overwhelmed life.

Choose Your Path : Consequential Thinking & Caring

Look before you Leap, Think before you Act ! These are the "pause" buttons you need to hit when you engage our emotions in your decision making. An life is full of decisions, little ones, big one, huge one and even the decision not to make a decision ! When you "know yourself" more, you understand your emotions, recognize their patterns, navigate yourself through them to reach your objectives and keep "Choosing for Yourself", the tools you need to manage and drive your emotional cars.

You need to begin as a learner at the wheel of life and graduate to a mature driver of chance and change, thinking ahead of the traffic of the expectations of other people, planning your route to success. All the while watching the rear view mirror carefully as you peer ahead through the windscreen often fogged by the heat of your own and others emotions.

Consequential thinking of what lies ahead and what can happen from the choices you make, is a very useful state of mind to master. It helps clear the mist and fog of assumptions you may have made, now that reality is presenting itself to you more clearly.

Consequential thinking thus teaches you how to use your emotional competencies to steer clear of trouble and navigate to success.

Lead with the Heart : The Roots of Empathy

Dr. Dan Siegel says that "Empathy comes in many colours. Often you may think of your ability to see from another's perspective as the essence of social savvyness. Empathy goes beyond that and is the competence of making others "feel felt by you". It is a way of sensing if their feelings are in tune with you, and that you can resonate with their own inner life.

This emotional empathy enables you to feel close and comforted, to sense that others are connected to you beneath and beyond the logic of rational thinking, and that you are concerned about each other, have compassion for each other's pain and take joy in each other's triumphs." This makes empathy the vibrant rainbow in the emotional sky of our connected lives.

Give Generously of Yourself : Live & Transform Life Everyday

"Success in life does not necessarily mean acquisition of wealth. Success in life is said to be a state of being when one can come home at the end of the day satisfied with what one has done, being able to put your head on your pillow and have a sound sleep and … wake up the next day realizing that you are a happy individual, not only because you have found happiness for yourself, but in the process of one day's work, you have given happiness to your spouse, to your children, to your family, to your neighbours and to the world at large." Can you make this your mission too - to live and transform everyday life , everyday

Reflecting, Activation, Action

For each of the Six Reflections, make a weekly Reflection Journal of your thoughts, feelings and actions

Convert as many into actual actions. Journal how these actions worked for you.

Observe yourself rather than judge. Become curious about how you can influence others to join you on your journey.

Here are a few practical ways. Choose some of them till you can do all of them with ease over time.

MEET YOURSELF TO KNOW YOURSELF

1. Maintain a Journal or Diary and write down the emotions you experienced during the day (without judgment or blame)

2. Write down what you are grateful for having in your life

3. Make a list of what you want or desire

4. Make a list at the end of each week, the habitual emotions you have experienced across the week repeatedly, then do this month-wise too. Do not justify the emotions.

5. Write down your feelings (not your judgments or opinions) about – a) Your Work b) Your Team c) Your Boss d) Your Clients/Customers e) your Spouse f) Your

Children g) Your Parents h) Your Career i) Your Future j) Yourself

6. Seek Feedback regularly on your behavior, performance and relationships form those you value and those than matter

UNDERSTAND YOURSELF BETTER

1. Write down a list of your Talents

2. Write down what motivates you about yourself (what are you proud of ?)

3. Write down how these Talents / Traits have helped you and helped others

4. Write down a truthful positive description of yourself and read this aloud 5 times every morning

5. Write down every day any situation (and associated feelings) you are frustrated with- see how you can positively REFRAME your thoughts and feelings about it by – taking Ownership, Stopping Blaming Life or Others or Yourself, De-personalizing it (stop self-talk where you choose to be a Victim)

6. Reflect on your Positive Affirmation of yourself as in point #4 above and think how the "Positive You" will now handle this situation

CHOOSE YOUR PATH - LEARN CONSEQUENTIAL THINKING & NAVIGATION

1. In your Journal, make a section for Consequences of Actions.

2. At the end of each week, review the week and write down 2 Positive and 2 Negative Consequences of your behavior – each from Work and Home

3. Write down the a) Situation b) the People involved c) your Feelings (Emotions) at that time d) Your Actions e) Consequences of your Actions / Inaction

4. Ask yourself the following questions and write the answers down briefly:

A What am I thinking NOW about what happened?

B What 3 – 4 emotions am I experiencing NOW when I think about what happened?

C What do I WANT to happen?

D How am I blocking my own path to what I want?

E What do I need to do Differently?

GIVE GENEROUSLY OF YOURSELF. LEAD WITH EMPATHY

Empathy begins with being a good and genuinely interested listener.

1. Name 5 colleagues and 5 customers (or 5 vendors or 5 channel partners) you deal with regularly and write down what you wish to know more about them and their concerns.

2. Keep 1 or 2 pages for each of these 10 people and make it a point to fill in every week, some info about each of them.

3. Write 1 point (for each person) every week on how you can show more concern specific to their needs and practice it as often as possible during the week.

4. Next week write another point, practice and reflect on how the relationship is changing.

5. Re-read your "Life Goal" statement - a statement of Personal Purpose which connects with the State of the World and practice it with these 10 people.6. After every month add 2 more people to the list and continue

9

THE STREET CLOTHES OF RESPECT

A COMMONPLACE WORD THAT PACKS A POWERFUL PUNCH !

I am sure you have used this word many times in your life. It is also probably a value you have been advised to embody or one that you advise others to act with.

What is Respect and what's the fuss about it ?

"Respect, also called esteem, is a positive feeling or action shown towards someone or something considered important, or held in high esteem or regard."
Source : Wikipedia

Respect is probably the most understood value in action ! Aha ! In action ?

I would like to go somewhat beyond what Respect most often shows up as, in behaviour.

What would Respect look like on the streets of everyday life ?

How would we recognize it ?

What clothes does Respect wear ?

Can we wear them too ?

Well, here is what it could be.

The Street Clothes of Respect

Reciprocity and Responsiveness

Reciprocity and responsiveness needs to be graciously active and alive in a relationship. *It is the very fabric of the street clothes or respect.*

Turn this inwards into yourself as Regard. How much do we regard ourselves ? Do we really matter to ourselves? *This is the aura or perfume we wear of Self*

Respect. Every element of Respect which follows must first be applied to ourselves.

Empathic Engagement

Empathy is about caring enough to be available to let people know you acknowledge and value them, especially when they feel most vulnerable and emotionally frail. *Empathy does one significant thing. It does away with judgement and replaces it with curiosity and unconditional care.*

In the midst of the storm of sheer stress of competitiveness, volatility of the playing field, crashing economies, collapsing success strategies, complex and carefully formulated algorithms gone haywire. *Empathy is the Mind-Spa* to soak and calm fevered judgement, anger, guilt, shame and blame.

Empathetic engagement is what brings the soul to the surface. The resilience and coherence of the mind and heart. To courageously build choices patiently with optimism. Accompanied by the warmth of compassion. *It's always recognized in the vibrant yet deep colours of your street clothes of Respect.*

Supportive Space

When was the last time you sensed this ? How did it feel ? To have someone just hold that space for you to gather your thoughts and emotions and find your sense of purpose and direction.

Without judgement. Without advice. With empathy. With patience. With consideration for both *stated and unstated personal and emotional boundaries*. With caring acknowledgement of both strengths and also vulnerabilities. With willingness to be with you especially when you can not possibly contribute back.

Supportive Space are the hands that hold your heart. It is the comforting innerwear that clothes you in the most unpretentious and invisible way.

Promises Practiced

Stephen Covey wrote about Emotional Bank Accounting being the accumulation of small positive deposits made in each relationship. Keeping small promises is one of these small yet significant deposits.

Promises practiced is about putting everyday promises into practice. Little things. Like calling back. Coming on time. Showing up for the other. Being available. Offering help and acting on it. Taking ownership of shared responsibilities. Owning up for lapses and making up for them.

Promises practiced are those comfortable shoes that help you walk your talk. Take you the extra mile. Put a spring in your step and add strength to your stride.

Expectations Managed

What do you really want in a relationship ? What would make you feel that the other person cares ?

Investing in a relationship, emotionally and intentionally, creates greater awareness of the touchstones of each relationship, the patterns producing pain which need to be broken and reformed, the options available or choices which can be created.

Shared expectations management are the adjustable hats or caps we wear, share and gift to each other too.

It fits best when our expectations are acted on with reciprocity and responsiveness, engage the hearts of people in understanding them with empathy and supports the space in which expectations are struggling for visible form and articulate expression.

The sweat band of these hats tell stories of the everyday sweet sweat equity we put into our relationships as often as we can.

It says " You matter to me. And I shall always strive to give you, what you want from me. To be who you need me to be. Will you do the same for me ?"

Communicating Authentically

Underpinning all aspects of every relationship is Trust. Not just the performance of the elements of Trust. But importantly, communicating trust.

By communicating honestly. By communicating our intentions. By communicating our vulnerabilities and fears. By communicating our expectations. By dropping those needless masks we wear, out of our need to project strength, prowess, capability and competence. Communicating Trust is achieved via Communicating our Authenticity.

Communicating Authentically is the hallmark of transparency. Transparency unashamedly declares our vulnerabilities. We are all too human more often than we wish to be. And it's no sin to declare our utter human-ness. *We are okay being "extra-ordinary". The infinite power of naked ordinary-ness lies in its acceptance.*

Time (making & giving)

All of us make the time for what really matters to us. Yet we catch ourselves saying we don't have time to spare for others. Even those who seem to matter to our lives.

The hard truth is that none of any of the street clothes of respect can be worn, unless we first wear the watch of time on our wrist. But then, the irony is that we must give it away every hour every day. Yes. To ourselves too. A man with no time for himself cannot give any away !

Our lives are time shared. We don't live fully when we live in the narrow speed lane of our own share of this time.

Making and giving time to create, grow and nurture relationships is like parenting. If you don't invest the time and energy into it, the child will grow anyway. And we shall pay a bitter and painful price for what it grows into.

Make the time willingly, with grace, clothe it everyday on the streets of life with respect and more time shall be made and given back. Especially when our time has finally come.

Summing up, the street clothes of respect when worn well clothes not just the wearer but also miraculously everyone the wearer embraces and enfolds into a growing, graceful and gracious life.

KEY ACTIONS :

Write a note to yourself based on what you've read , setting out a R-E-S-P-C-T Blueprint!

10
RELATING WITH EMOTIONAL PURPOSE

EMOTION IS THE EQUAL PARTNER OF PURPOSE

Visible or invisible, conscious or sub conscious, acceptable or unacceptable, every relationship has a purpose.

When that is gone, so is the relationship.

Emotion is indeed the equal partner of purpose. Although quite often, emotion being more experienced in the mind and body, may actually obscure sighting the purpose itself. Interestingly, when the emotion runs dry, so does the relationship. If you are engaged more with the emotion than the purpose which produces or accompanies the emotion, well, it may just leave you stranded and adrift, when it runs out.

So Love, for example, and not Lust which is often confused with Love, one of the biggest human emotions, is not the purpose of the relationship. But as an emotion, it's quite overwhelming. Love is often called the seventh wave in a sea of emotions that floats the ship of purpose. Which could be the vision of life together, children, building a great future together, partnership, and so on. Love is the emotion that wraps the vision around the relationship. And holds it together.

So why would the emotional glue run dry ? And strangely, it quite often does, doesn't it ? Sometimes emotional glue is replaced with emotional dynamite !! That is enough to clue us into the insight that the original emotion has transferred out of the relationship, perhaps because either the vision has played out its course and the purpose fulfilled. Or, the vision has shifted or redirected elsewhere or even crumbled along the way. And the binding emotion has metamorphed into something else.

Like Love turning lukewarm, because of an anticipated shared future together with children, morphing into a future of two independent lives held together just by children or joint financial engagements or physical assets and investments; the relationship spiraling down to a necessary business partnership. Or terrible incompatibility with each other's habits, wants, needs or desires at close range can erode the vision crafting the very purpose of the relationship, with the core emotions then shifting to ones less binding. Maybe even more loosening to allow for breaking or unraveling of the relationship.

Have you experienced this in your lives? Has a relationship that enthralled and bound you now become less enchanting or even broken? Or has it improved? Did a mild emotion with loose ties turn into a burning flame? Did you find purpose shifting from casual to imperative? Or did a need that originally drove your purpose get fulfilled elsewhere?

What's the more powerful experience for you? And what does it tell you about how you have engaged with your life's purpose or purposes with the people you've enrolled?

We usually look for 6Rs in the performance of a relationship: *Role, Relevance, Resonance & Reciprocity, Rigour, Resilience and Results.* We can call the fulfilment of these, evolved purpose.

Role is the part your play, to fulfil the expectations of others in the relationship.

Relevance is about how much you matter and bring purpose and direction to the relationship

Resonance is whether you relate your needs and expectations well to others needs, expectations. How much you are in tune with the others in the relationship

Reciprocity goes hand in hand with Resonance and is about contributing as much as you receive from the relationship. The more wholesome and unconditional, the better

Rigour is the effort you put in to manage the relationship. It is not about labouring under a load, but actually about how much time and energy you invest willingly.

Resilience is ofcourse how much the relationship survives and thrives under pressure and strife.

Results is how everyone in the relationship views how it is working for them. It is especially measured in times of stress, strain, emergencies and circumstances which test the resilience of the relationship

All these together deliver what I like to call Evolved Purpose to the relationship. Or ***Emotional Evolved Purpose***, since our emotions continuously define this purpose.

So here is my question. Is there still enough evolved purpose to keep you in relationships which have served you well? Have you discovered or uncovered mistaken or neglected purpose along the way? Do you feel that maybe you, despite your best intentions, could not work with sufficient zeal and purpose towards your vision of the relationship? Have you begun to take the relationship for granted?

Are you on the road to make, mend, amend or break?

It hardly matters anymore in the present, what the past threw up. Especially when we understand that investing in the relationship is a continuous process, and some investments are either made incorrectly or insufficiently or timed badly.

Yet our egos are often in constant battle with what should have been. Who we are or not is then defined by our ego. So out of the window flies the original emotional evolved purpose. And in comes Ego with explosive emotional baggage which redefines, redirects, contorts and throttles our evolved purpose. Well and truly hijacked. The ghosts of the past are now here to haunt our future.

Being in the moment, is the most powerful way to exorcise the ghost of past perfidies. Let the past guide but not dictate the present. Look for past patterns that presently play out invisibly in crucial areas of your life .

It's probably good practice to pause and check for evidence of emotional evolved purpose in your relationships. If you find that evidence and the emotional partnership, you could consciously stroke the responsiveness of that relationship.

If you are struggling to find the evidence, maybe there is a tsunami of hidden emotions building in that sea !! Better get your relationships and partnerships to higher ground !! From there you can retrieve purpose or even redefine it.

Make up your mind and your heart about the energy you need to invest in the emotional purpose that drives each relationship. Release energies you have imprisoned in fatigued relationships to bring fresh perspective to fuel the true emotional purpose of your life.

Success in any area of life, depends on the quality of your relationships driving the results you desire and seek.

KEY ACTIONS :

Reflect on the 6Rs and write your own analysis of these for each of your significant relationships. At work and in your personal life as well

Make a remedial plan where necessary and a way to sustain and grow those relationships which are thriving. You may be surprised how near to breaking point some are, how much fuel in the tank from earlier investments has carried you further than expected. Becoming conscious of the state of these relationships, will certainly bring forth energized emotional evolved purpose in them.

11
YOU ARE APPROVED !
CERTIFIED , SIGNED AND STAMPED BY YOU !

The Seal of Approval is almost as coveted as the mysterious and elusive Holy Grail. Both are the result of Man's quest for "Divinity by Proximity" because possessing either would mean raising of the mere mortal to the realms of the supreme spirit. From nothingness to everything, finite to infinite, inconsequential to undeniably intrinsic, banished to proclaimed, wastrel to apostle, rejected to celebrated !

Ah ! Rejection, the scourge of mortal mankind. For no man is an island, therefore he must relate to others and integrate with the rest of the world. Which in many ways translates to being accepted and approved by others in order to develop competence in the area of interpersonal relationships. Wrong !

All of us undeniably need to be appreciated, which is a positive stroke to our sense of being and doing. Dependency on this need in order to feel better about ourselves is a disorder of rationality and often an emotional overrun stemming from a whole spectrum of causes. Let's take a look at some of them and see if we can figure a way to transcend these obstacles to a sense of self worth and equilibrium with the rest of the world.

We have been schooled to judge ourselves the ways others see us. Our education system itself unwittingly endorses this inequity, with our sense of competence and ability being judged by others in the close confines and constraints of an academic assessment of memory skills rather than processed thought, applied knowledge and competence to deliver. We ignore the multiple intelligences across which learning can be delivered and force-feed it in a manner which cannot possibly produce the best results.

Those who "beat the system" by mastering the manipulation of clear process flaws, such as offered by almost any coaching or tutorial class, are approved, whilst the real student of learning can often be denied approval or competitive levels of the certification of competences , which have not really been tested.

Collective experiences of being undervalued across life often find origins in the shrouding of one's capability in the advocated cloak of "humility" , a virtue we are told to hold dear by a generation of an old world , going into oblivion, as a guide to a new world they have barely experienced and an emerging world they could not possibly accept. Values and belief systems of a dated perception of reality, have contributed to our continued subscription to a single window of assessment of ourselves rather than a 360 degree multiple window assessment centre.

The overpowering need for approval from others has its roots in a deep scarring of a sense of self and an erosion of our deposits of self worth. Lack of approval or acceptance both direct and discreet is what we consider to be "rejection". But how bad is rejection and what does it really mean to us ?

"I take rejection as someone blowing a bugle in my ear to wake me up and get going, rather than retreat." Says the famous American actor Sylvester Stallone, true to his reel-life personas Rambo and Rocky Balboa

Rejection is a word we are plagued with because we have described it to ourselves as failure and we consider failure to be a destination rather than an event. To experience rejection is to experience failure – if viewed positively, this just means that somehow something we do, does not meet with what somebody expects or needs. It does not mean that we become useless or worthless. A one million dollar cheque given to a man too poor to have a bank account, does not make either the one million dollars less that what it is worth or the man poorer than he originally was. The inability to encash the cheque, simply suspends the delivery of wealth at that moment. It does not deny it. Self worth is the multi-million dollar potential we are all born with.

Each and every one of us is born priceless, and everyday we gain in value no matter what we do, simply because we are there to witness the day. We can deny the acceptance of the moment and embrace the rejection of those to come. Rejection at it's worst is a judgement of the past, not of the future. And since the future holds all the wealth we want or desire, what prevents us from going forward ? A fall in the past ? If all our futures were pinned on the "sins" of the past, we would not survive childhood.

Karl Stern the noted German-Canadian neurologist and psychiatrist puts rejection into succinct perspective when he says *"Psychoanalysis shows the human infant as the passive recipient of love, unable to bear hostility. Development is the learning to love actively and to bear rejection."*

So how do you get beyond the fear of rejection? Simple. Or is it ? Learn to love yourself. Which means, learn to appreciate yourself, concentrating on reframing your focus from what's wrong to what's right in your life, approving of yourself wholeheartedly, celebrating who you are, remembering we are all Work in Progress and that Perfection is an endeavour, a journey.

It is the journey that is significant, for the journey and not the pit-stops we make en-route, is the longest experience.

The next time you feel rejected, issue yourself a Certificate of Approval, signed and stamped by YOU! Encash your multi-million dollar future NOW!

12
RESOLVING IRRESOLUTE RESOLUTIONS

LIFE DEALS THE CARDS, WE SORT THEM INTO WINNING HANDS !

This book would not be complete without this success script ! The Energy of Our New Year Resolutions. Why we make them and must sustain them !

So why do we still make New Year Resolutions ? And still break them ? Is it just old "brainwired" habit, a ritual that routinely clicks into place ?

Lets ask a few obvious questions :

- Why make resolutions at all ?
- Why worry if we break them ?

- Why wait until New Year to do so ?
- How relevant are our resolutions to our real problems ?
- How researched are our resolutions that they deliver significantly?
- Can resolutions be changed as the situation changes ?
- Should resolutions be changed anyway ?
- How important are resolutions to altering our lives driven by destiny ?

We can go on of-course with innumerable questions to numb our mind and senses to the subject, so that we can then let it wither away from our zone of concern, leave alone our zone of influence and action.

Let's therefore see some of the logic behind New Year's Resolutions :

- The New Year is when we clear the page of life and start afresh.
- The New Year has a common sense of renewal and resurgence which can find an emotional tie with our resolutions
- The New Year denies the seamlessness of time that chains us down to our committed lives and helps get us of the old hook.

- Every New Year seems to indicate a turning or tipping point in life. Resolutions made at the tipping or turning point are usually made with far greater insight than when made routinely.
- Making resolutions are great fun. They allow us to air our dreams. Dreams given oxygen can live longer than those suffocated.
- Resolutions are a release of the soul. We can unburden all our guilt of the past and commit them to the future, where we believe we can be more powerful to handle it.
- Resolutions tell us what we really want, but cannot seem to get.
- Resolutions are a way of making us conscious of what's blocking our path to success or happiness.
- Breaking resolutions are surprisingly an expected event, as the deeply rooted behavioral shift that is expected to accompany the resolution to implementation is often too difficult to accomplish in one go.

So what are we left with ????

Let us see if we can make some sense of all of this.

According to me, I could not agree more with the answers above.

It is difficult to give up old behavior we are emotionally attached to or have found even secret comfort with, in favour of a shining new but difficult-to-do behavior which creates extreme discomfort. It's like wanting to shift home to a new fantastic place but have nothing to do with the back-breaking and often heart-breaking clearing, sorting, disposing and moving process at all ! But at least we now have embedded the desire to move. And we have an address.

I love making resolutions at New Year and I am delight at breaking some of them too. Funny or crazy or perhaps both ? But I do learn from them to some extent. This learning I fill into the gaps of my existing goal sheet and then it makes more sense.

The Blueprint of my life is a Five Pointed Star of Purpose and Direction.

I regularly set time framed meaningful, measurable and monitored goals in each area.

Every New Year resolution I make, must somehow connect with my 5 point Star. I must see the connect and deeply desire the difference it will make to my Star. *This is the key to keeping or breaking resolutions made*. It's all about how much we really want it at the conscious and unconscious level of our thinking process. Resolutions reframe and redirect our efforts to meet our goals.

The blueprint of my life however is not set at New Year's eve. It is an ongoing process of refining my dream. Sometime back I sat down and asked myself what goals I had in life and what was the quality of my goals ? I realized much to my shock, that my busy life was being run by happenstance rather than design. It took me a while to lay out a design and I have found this useful. May I offer this to you to see if you would like to try it out too.

The Tip of my Star is my Life Goal , **My Purpose** or my ultimate dream. I do not change my Life Goal but continue to validate and qualify it, to keep deriving a greater sense of purpose to my life, in order to set direction

Around my Purpose, revolve my Personal Goals which support it, such as Health, Relationships, Social, Lifestyle, Habits some of which may also reflect in the categories below.

The other Four Points of my Five Pointed Star are:

My Career Goals (My job, my designation, my advancement in my field, my professional path)

My Professional Equity Goals (My History Sheet : What makes me Good and Reliable- the reasons why someone would invest in me namely my knowledge, skills, competences, qualifications, additional certification and so on.

My Brand Equity Goals (My Unique Selling Proposition, What I Want to be Known For, My Mindshare Flag – just as any Brand has to be developed to be an automatic choice of the market right across the segment)

My Leadership Goals (My ability to Lead, Influence, Impact and Inspire others – one does not need hierarchy to hold us hostage to the power of leadership, for leadership needs to be a way of life, anywhere in the pyramid of society or the organization)

At New Year's eve, I allow my soul to set itself free to quest beyond the blueprint. To light up the new canvass with the same brilliance that the New Year seems to hold.

I thrill at the colourful sparkles and fountains of radiance that my resolutions bring to my trusty Star of Life. And some of these glistening shards of my extended reality glitter on my Star as the year goes through. While some of them sprinkle fairy dust around the place. For even in trying and not quite succeeding, the journey itself is blessed and leaves a comet like trail to my shining star.

For EVERY NEW YEAR to come, may I wish you all a wonderful shining STAR of Hope and Promise, complete with glorious comet trails of glittering resolutions that fill your heart with as great a delight as the shining promise the future holds.

KEY ACTION:

Make your very own FIVE Pointed Star of Life with Goals that support and lead you to your Purpose.

Write it down here !

BONUS
A PRESSURE COOKED LIFE
A POTFUL OF PARENTING GOULASH

The children of today and their parents are subject to innumerable stressors and pressure-cooker circumstances of a competitive-crazy world. Managing daily life itself is a stupendous task. There seems to be no time or patience for any thing or for that matter any person out of control or even out of the careful alignment with our regulated lives. The careless and carefree child, both real and the one in all of us, must conform or convert to a sedate straight-jacketed adult.

Living on the leading edge of life in today's rushed and rough times, involves both parents being actively engaged with careers that turn in the money to fund the household and lifestyle economies. Growing awareness of competitive careers and advancement vistas in the great big span of working life, has helped cast the dragnet over even the most the unsuspecting home-warming individual.

Bounding out of the couch of comfort, both men and women are brandishing degrees and skills that lay claim to jobs and careers that demand an all-consuming attention absorbing time and life like a gigantic blotting paper.

Regulation, regimentation, rigour are the watchwords of a timetabled life , driven by the need for bringing certainty and predictability to an anticipated incredible combo of a see-sawing roller-coaster life.

Instead of creative-constructs we seek regulated-regularity. The happy lull of mediocrity is the way to an undisturbed life. But ever so often Life has other plans....

What happens when we are faced with uncertainty , when our time tables have no meaning, when our plans find no place to unfold, when our carefully crafted lives are ripped apart by reality ?

What happens when all this happens because of our children ? Or the pressures put on our children ??

Such as competitive social lifestyles, expensive gadgets & gizmos, tuitions, peer-pressure, overly competitive exam pressures, study-load, rivalries at school / college, victimization by teachers, failure, fear-of-failure, success itself, substance abuse like smoking, drugs, alcoholism, absenteeism, sickness – real and imagined............ ???

Parenting can be a bizarre experience for both the parent and the child. Almost all parents, teachers and tutors expect the child to develop in to a superhuman composition of talent, knowledge, skills, competence along with vision, foresight, clarity of purpose, ambition, all neatly folded and pressed into the sharp edges of the shining blade of the sword of success. All this must of-course fit into the pre-constructed timetable of the mentor, unfortunately soon to be tormentor !

Parenting from afar, remote controlling results, financing concern, and funding the future is the order of the day today. But where is the Love ? Where is the Care and Compassion ? Where is the Connect between lives ? Where is the Soul of the family ?

The expected brusque answer you invariably get is : Where is the Time ? Aha ! Find Purpose and the Means usually follows. Alas, the Means is oft the End !

So here is a potful of parenting goulash for the modern family meal:

1. **BE INVOLVED** : Decide to set aside time to connect with your children every day. Get to know your child and let your child discover you. Give the gift of togetherness, it is far more precious than any other.

2. **CONNECT** : Be a parent and a friend – and draw the line clearly between the two. Shuffle the cards and no matter which falls first, you will always deal a good hand. This makes the transition easier as you both grow.

3. **VALUE** : Always value the child. The messenger is sometimes the hapless carrier of an incorrect message.. Reinforce your belief in the person even when you have to admonish the behavior.

4. **CO-CREATE** : Take a personal interest in shaping, not shoving, the child's knowledge, skills and abilities, on a regular basis.

5. **BE PATIENT** : Do not expect miracles to happen. Give the child time to grow and learn. Do not rob your child of the delightful process of growing and learning, just as you cannot hasten the metamorphosis of the caterpillar into a butterfly.

6. **SUPPORT & GUIDE** : Be available to nurture the growth of your child- mental, physical, spiritual and emotional. It is important to move from choking controls

of the regulating parent to performing as a nurturing parent within the footprint of the controlling parent. Which means while setting clear and enforceable rules, throw yourself into enabling and supporting performance within the rules.

7. **COMMIT** : Make a promise and keep it. Let you child see your commitment to the family. Demonstration of commitment is a sure fire way to build trust. Commitment means never giving up on promises, goals, dreams and especially people.

8. **LEAD BY EXAMPLE** : What you want your child to do, is best reflected in what you do and how you do it too. Role modeling is one of the most powerful ways to help your child grow by your own demonstration of the "right" way. We all remember what we see and practice. So give it a go, it will help you too !

9. **FORGIVE** : Learn to be generous. Bearing grudges and wielding the club of reform is hardly the way to conduct life. If you have to threaten , be prepared to carry out the threat, and bear the consequences. So wherever possible, forgive the messenger, and correct the message.

10 **HAVE FUN** : The bottom line here is so often in the red. What is life without a good dose of fun. Let your child grow in the sunshine of love and fun. Let the children of this world want to live on.

Now apply all of these TEN INGREDIENTS of the Parenting Goulash RECIPE to your TEAM at Work!

The Menu is the Meal. Bon Appétit !!

ABOUT THE AUTHOR

Professionally Certified Coach (**Results Coaching Systems @ 2008- International Coach Federation certified & Professional Coach Certification @ Coaching Lighthouse @ 2019**)

Internationally Certified ENNEAGRAM Personality Profiling @ 2009(Certified by Jerome Wagner)

Internationally Certified Emotional Intelligence Practitioner, EQ Vital Signs Consultant, Certified EQ – Assessor & Coach @ **2010, 2011, 2012, 2013** (Certified by Six Seconds , California)

Internationally Certified MiND Practitioner @ **2016** (Certified by MyBrain International Limited, UK)

DEXTER J VALLES

A Profile

An International Business Professional, a Life & Executive Coach, *Acclaimed Corporate Master Trainer & a Professor of Management Studies* , across an extensive career founded over an absorbing 32 years with Global and Indian markets

Dexter is considered one of India's leading EQ consultants, specializing in the crucial area of *neuroscience based Emotional Intelligence EQ competencies* applied to Life & Leadership. He is a multi-certified EQ Practitioner, EQ Assessor and Organizational EQ Vital Signs consultant helping people and organizations connect life & work competencies to hidden behavioural drivers

Coaching has been a pursuit of passion for the past 10 years, ever since certifying as a Coach first in 2008. The desire was to enable people reach their goals way beyond the *"classroom of learning"* into the streets of life and the aspirations at their workplaces.

Empaneled as Lead Learning Facilitator, over 20 years Dexter has facilitated and coached dreams and desires, developing competence of several thousands of participants across the globe through innumerable training workshops with several key Indian and Multinational Corporate Houses

Dexter's VIDEO Talks

We invite you to look at these interesting videos

Perceiving Reality
https://youtu.be/fG4kGk_IOiA

Perception and Reality are often debated to understand what's really true. Is there anything like Reality? Is it all Perception. Well it all depends on how they matter and to whom. Does Reality exist by itself? Is information and data useful if not processed in context to a framework? The same goes for Reality! Perceiving Reality on our own context sets up the world to be judged by us. Based on our assumptions and filters of our experiences. We have an image or perception or preconceived expectation of ourselves to begin with, others around us, how the world works and how it should. All this makes up for an interesting life executing our judgements and decisions on which we act.

Engaging the Energy of Life
https://youtu.be/4y35QrrO8qg

We drag ourselves around our lives with just about enough energy to reach the end of the day. How much are we paying Mindful attention to what our energy is creating or blocking? Developing energy that vibrates at higher frequencies creates positive attraction, attention, connection and influence. We create the energy field we operate within and connect with the world. And therefore we create the world we live in.

Connecting with Purpose Everyday

https://youtu.be/fU0I5YUo8hc

Everyday we are busy with the actions that make up life. Our goals and plans collide with the reality of each day. We strive, we cope, we do. Endlessly. But how much of it has meaning ? How does it connect with our purpose. The reason we live. The person we are. Who we want to truly be. Can everyday contribute in a small way to our future ? Can we get to that happy place where we know everyday that we have done something that is worthwhile and meaningful? Can we communicate that to ourselves to energize our lives, in place of the exhaustion and exasperation with our" human doing" rather than "human being" !

Leading Success with your Heart

https://youtu.be/TPadHbXiBt8

What's your Mantra for Success ? How do you balance Power, Success, Performance and People ? Merging the Mind with the Heart allows one to lead with Competence and also with Compassion, Courage and Character. It helps deliver outstanding results and create powerful relationships. Aligning Vision and Purpose with managing People, Performance and Practices. Coherence of Head, Heart and Hands.

The Sigma of Presentation Skills

https://youtu.be/SI-EzwnHm6o

Make a great first impression ! But how?? !! Butterflies in the stomach, the mind blanking out, being transfixed or stuttering at the start could be your doom ! So use the SIGMA way to make a great start. One which will put you at ease and give you the confidence to make a great presentation. Of course there's a lot more to Presentation Design and Delivery. We shall keep that for another time !!

Communicating Assertively
https://youtu.be/fWIKh-3eOH8

Our relationships influence the nature and quality of our communication. Assertiveness as a way of life is about being clear, firm and fair in communicating our intentions first and our behaviour based on securing an equitable result for everyone as much as possible. It's not possible to do this all the time, but if it is a large part of how we behave, people will ultimately respond in similar ways. Investing in relationships is a good way to call on them to address the needs of all people in the relationship. This does not mean that new or brief relationships need witness a free-for-all brawl or mute acceptance. It just means that when we practice assertiveness enough, it comes through in even the smaller moments of life. Our intentions get curated to a level at which even if communication breaks down, people feel safe enough to continue the conversation.

Live Life Beyond Learning & Assessments
https://youtu.be/jbi6CBI9K2E

Many among us would have received feedback on ourselves. As students our report cards served as feedback. As corporate citizens it's our performance assessment and conversations with our seniors. As adult learners we get various inputs from learning programs, learning models, audits and assessments - psychometric and others. Putting it all together can be quite a task. Perhaps we should just be listening in rather than being handcuffed to these. Filling in the blanks into our blindside can be useful. Does not mean we discard everything we know or think we know about ourselves. Rather we can use such inputs to also clarify, validate and curate the info we have. Remember that our lives are across a canvas far greater than the assessment windows and models which look at certain specific aspects of our lives in an interesting and insightful way. We are larger than the data. And the context within which we operate our lives is more dynamic. Let the context not suffer from the content. Yet let the content inform the context too!

Masks & Me
https://youtu.be/AogKMdbzAv8
Do you wear a mask? Yes we all do for different reasons. Most of them are to project an image. How authentic are we when for every good reason we project who we wish to be than who we really are? What is the benefit and how much does it cost us? How can we close the gap between the authentic self and the projected self? When can we evolve to authentically be the mask we wear?

Learn Life's Lessons Everyday
https://youtu.be/ptZP3zaMsCg
Everyday provides us moments of truth which indicate lessons we can use to make life better. Even the smallest lesson can turn to deliver the greatest benefit. How much are you paying attention to what your life and experiences are telling you?

Dance to Lifes' Music
https://youtu.be/HFZFB3HnO28
Everyday we live, we learn. Capture each lesson consciously. Share it with others. We live very different lives but surprisingly have very similar needs. The music of our lives can help other people dance through theirs !

Life is All Around You. Are you Present ?
https://youtu.be/LDuuuECIGd8

AT THE STEERING WHEEL OF LIFE

We hurry through life, trying to get to the other side. Success and Happiness. They are all somehow only in the Future. Can we notice the moment we are in ? What are we ignoring and perhaps losing in our race to the future ? When that too becomes the present, will we race through it too ? Arriving numbed and dazed at the end of life ?

The Steering Wheel of Life-Edited
https://youtu.be/W0KdbtKwX6Q
Do you feel in control of life only when you are driving it? Are your hands locked on the steering wheel. Are you driving blind through traffic. Is there a chance you could fall asleep at the wheel? How do we deal with handing over the wheel to someone else? Is it always our car and our destination that matters? What do we need to consider on the shared journey of life such that we live as fully as possible in the moment whilst creating the future?

Steering Wheel & You !
https://youtu.be/yr4UTMy_UJ4
At the Steering Wheel of Life are you driving people Nuts??!! Is your focus so single minded that you drive by the moment and the magic of the process to a destination that denies you the journey itself? What does it mean to be obsessed with controlling the wheel of your life and all those in your car? At work how connected are you with your team? Are they empowered to drive your car? At home, are you so fixated at the wheel that it doesn't matter where others want to go, as long as they are going with you? How much will it take to unlock your grip from the wheel and embrace the journey together with others?

Driving Performance Excellence-Edited
https://youtu.be/FKHxgvzxWt8
Four Key Performance Drivers explained.

Our success lies in how we perform. How we perform lies in what drives us. What drives us depends on what motivates us and others. Motivation depends a lot on our emotional energy and our relationships with people we wish to impact with our performance ! We take a look at 4 Key Drivers : Communicating with Impact & Influence, Managing a Changing Environment, Performing through People with Empathy and Making a Personal Difference.

The Art of Winning Arguments
https://youtu.be/Z5xqVtBUNZc
Most of the time in the rush to decide things, our conversations, discussions and debates turn into Win-Lose Arguments. There are victors and there are the vanquished. Relationships fall apart. So perhaps we need to revisit the words we are using to describe these conversations in our minds. The way we position ourselves. The stances we adopt. The emotions were engage with. And the traffic jams of our collective egos we are stuck in.

Winning "Arguments" without Losing Relationships. Needs you to Change your Language, Reframe Communication, Take Responsibility, Enlist support, Engage Empathy and convert arguments into productive high energy courageous conversations.

Asserting your EQ
https://youtu.be/LHwsTi9p0Q0

Assertiveness is the key to EQ. Communicating is crucial to managing Relationships and Results. Communicating with Emotional Balance is how we demonstrate emotional intelligence. Powerful, trustworthy, authentic and reliable relationships help us get to the results we desire. Assertiveness is a critical milestone on pathway to an EQ life!

The Code of the Road
https://youtu.be/pPvjbB_A7zk

The roads we travel on and the traffic we negotiate everyday are uncannily like life itself. Here we take a look at what quick lessons we can learn on the roads of life and put them to work in life itself.
Music credit : Dreamy Dreamers by Samsung Galaxy A50s mobile phone video editing software

Claim your Rightful Life
https://youtu.be/1TIBeKJloml

Little things do matter. The permissions you give define the quality of your life. Announce your Life is about claiming your right to a life that is fair, just, equitable and civil. It's about setting your boundaries. We teach others how to treat us by the way we treat ourselves. We need to stand up, smile and say something! Because it matters !!

Who are you ?
https://youtu.be/i1MdAlr9Alc

We often define our lives by what we do. Yet we are not truly products of our profession or qualifications or achievements. That's why some people great success stories are riddled with doubt and unhappy with their lives. Finding out the answer to Who You Are can help find Purpose and redefine your life. Or of course endorse your life. Either way, it's good to answer the question Who Are You !

Engaging EQ Energy
https://youtu.be/b9M-VapoAN4

This is the first Episode in the series Engaging EQ Energy. It's about understanding Emotional Intelligence, the role of emotions themselves, the EQ Framework and How one can engage the 3 Pursuits of the EQ Competences as defined by Six Seconds, California, USA, world leaders in the study and application of EQ.

LESSONS FROM THE CROSS OF CRISIS
https://youtu.be/wXLvfAi5mxl

Every crisis has several lessons to learn from. Currently the world is plunged into the chaos of the Coronavirus Crisis. Our very existence is threatened. Panic has taken over the reins of what we once knew to be a regulated, planned and organized life. Pressing the Pause Button has put the world face to face with the most dreadful reality of our times. Yet there are compelling lessons to learn as we survive this gut wrenching turbulence. Five Lessons emerge with practical wisdom which we can harness to negotiate our passage through life.

Making Relationships Count
https://youtu.be/qIKMHckXWW0

We are often held hostage by our friendships and relationships. Burdened by the responsibility of managing the imbalances and inequities of the relationship. Taking the blame in order to keep the peace. An unfair friendship is destructive. Manipulative relationships make doormats of people who are unwilling to call out the unfairness and have conversations about how it needs to be. Beware of being a victim or victimizing others in friendships where too much is being asked of the other almost all of the time.

Fingerprinting Success
https://youtu.be/QCucf5n-1G0

Just as our fingerprint is an unique identification of each of us as individuals, success too has an unique DNA or Fingerprint of how we engage our Values, our Goals and our Emotions which hold them together and give them life and direction. It's all in our hands, literally and figuratively!! Here we look at an interesting way to count our Values and Goals on our fingers and look at what we hold in the palms of our hands. Our Core Values and Our Vision which together script the Legacy of our Lives

REWIRING Life Beyond COVID-19
https://youtu.be/co_uA-fZoGA

The world is under siege and we are besieged with the fear of the unknown and unseen. Never before have we had to change the context of our lives so dramatically. We can take this time and opportunity to rewire and reimagine our lives beyond the uncertainty and disruption we are struggling to live through.

To REFRAME our lives is to recreate the context within which we operate, moving from Panic & Paralysis to Productivity.

R : Review & Reflect on what are thoughts are in the moment
E : Engagement Levels of our Emotions and Actions
F : Focus on FIVE important issues
R : Draw up a Rewiring Plan.
A : Activate the Plan
M : Measure Progress, Mend the Plan to work better
E : Educate, Enlarge & Energise your Reframed life

Locked Down & Locked Into Life
https://youtu.be/GIqaSCqqw4w

Learning to deal with the lockdown allows us to revisit our lives. And learn as students of the game, once again. Stay Home Stay Safe and Stay a Student of Life. This is Life sending us Back to School !

Living a Re-Loaded Life !
https://youtu.be/0VuMZWsGlps

The old ways die away as we learn to cope in the new world of 2020. This is a year we shall never forget. Stories shall be told of how we fought the Coronavirus and survived How the world stopped its mad dash to an insane future. How we recreated or were forced to recreate the world which we had dismantled and almost destroyed. Let's make sure we are part of that story. Let's give ourselves reasons to succeed Time to think how we need to revitalize old ways, values and behaviours to succeed in the new context that this scourge has thrown to recast the very vitality of life

Lockdown into your Legacy_ Rewrite your Story
https://youtu.be/7NZ_KXPEPPk

Use the coronavirus lockdown to look into rewriting the story of your life. Thread the significant moments of your life and see how your story had developed and defined life. Most of us have lived significant lives in many ways. Let's take that forward and leave a legacy. Something that lives beyond us as a gift to those who follow. This year 2020 is a landmark year in human history. Let it scare us to survive and thrive with renewed vigour and vitality. Let new powerful stories emerge beyond the lockdown ! Unlock the amazing stories from rest of your life !

The Power of Your Life Story !
https://youtu.be/n-54JHAgrF0

Our life is on Pause. It is the perfect gift of time and opportunity to look into rewriting the story of your life. Stitch the significant moments of your life driven by powerful emotions and see how your story had developed and defined life. What is the DNA of your life ? How is it going to help you ? This year 2020 is a landmark year in human history. Let new powerful stories emerge beyond the lockdown ! Emerge from the shadows to the light of the life of the future you are scripting today.

You can contact Dexter Valles here

DEXTER JOHN VALLES
CEO & Managing Consultant, Valmar International
Founder Director, The EQ Legion of India

Facebook
https://www.facebook.com/dexvalles
LinkedIn
https://www.linkedin.com/in/dextervalles
Twitter @dynamodex
Website 1
http://www.valmarinternational.com
Website 2
https://dextervalles.wixsite.com/website
Email : dexter@valmarinternational.com

Credits and references

Stephen Covey : 7 Habits of Highly Effective People (Emotional Bank Accounting)

Six Seconds www.6seconds.org The EQ Network. World leaders in Emotional Intelligence (EQ) – The EQ KCG Model and EQ Competencies

BOOKS BY THIS AUTHOR

INSPIRED BY THE HOLY SPIRIT

Available on www.amazon.com in Kindle and Paperback

The Butterfly Blueprint

Managing Transformative Change

Dexter Valles

THE BUTTERFLY BLUEPRINT
Managing Transformative Change

Metamorphosis is an incredibly fascinating journey of transitioning the ordinary caterpillar to a magnificent butterfly! It needs patience and care. Just as our own life must go through metamorphosis from helplessness to strength, from being unskilled and inept to being skilled and agile! Yet in our impatience we often wake up the Caterpillar in ourselves and others too, halfway through the metamorphosis, hoping that the butterfly within has already formed

Even before any of the magic has been displayed, we want this butterfly to grow its wings and fly. Our competitive speeding world in which we live today, brings us breathlessly close to the threshold of destroying the cocoon and the magical metamorphosis within it.
The cocoon after all, is that fragile vehicle and the extraordinarily painstaking process which transforms the Ugly Caterpillar into the Beautiful Butterfly.

Every caterpillar must bide its' time to be born a butterfly. The butterfly too, must be released from the memories of the cocoon, to fly gracefully in fields of flowers. The lessons from the cocoon are now invisible part of butterfly beauty and grace. That's the Butterfly Blueprint ! The Cocoon meets the Sky !

This book deals with this journey in Four Parts. Beginning with the Caterpillar, it's Metamorphosis, and finally the Butterfly ! We also look at the role of emotions accompanying the journey of the Butterfly Blueprint. To converge the Blueprint to everyday actions and advice, we Engage the Blueprint into FIVE Focus Areas in the Butterfly Blueprint's Flight

The Code of the Road

Navigating Life's Traffic Lanes

Dexter Valles

THE CODE OF THE ROAD
Navigating Life's Traffic Lanes

This book is a product of my everyday life, driving around in the heavily congested roads of my beloved city Mumbai in INDIA

I would end my day feeling an overwhelming rush of mixed emotions and found it really hard to shrug off the strong connections to everyday Life ! As I reflected on what I could learn from these experiences, interesting relationships began to form and make strange sense to me.

All travelers have encountered Roadblocks along their journeys. The 5 Road Block Lessons offer interesting insight into the usefulness of Roadblocks on the Road of Life. Navigating Life's Traffic Lanes takes you through 12 Lane Laws of Life each translated into a cryptic Life Lesson.

The Road of Life as you shall discover, is governed by The Code of the Road. The book takes you on a road trip through three segments – Your Car, The Road and The Code putting it all together in a delightful summary called You, The Road and the Code. Enjoy the Ride !

CONNECTED TO SOUL

Igniting Human Spirit with Purpose

This book explores the essence of life and the human spirit connected to the soul. That eternal part of us which ignites our purpose and passion. This creates meaning drawn from what we do and allows us leave a Legacy. This Legacy rides forward on that fuel of Purpose with Passion long after we have stopped stoking the fire ourselves.

 Man is eternally in search of two major engines to drive life. The Engines of Purpose and Provision. These create direction and meaning. The truth is that one does not often find both together. Yet either one has the power to deeply engage the human spirit.

Engaging Energy or Passion would depend on where the engagement lies. Together these engines enable us engage the incredible and enormous power of an ignited life!

The journey of this book winds across 3 Parts. Each Part has 4 Ways of looking at the theme of that part. The chapters in each part describe their story of this book in their own unique ways. As if each chapter is written from a different view of life. In a way, as a reader you get 12 different views of the book, almost just like life is most of the time. Together they bring to the reader, the essence of the entire story of the book itself.

FLAWED yet PRECIOUS

Leading a Sparkling Life

As time flows by, we often look back at all the years gone by, and strive to understand what life has taught us. What can we do better? What would really need to be New in the coming Year?? What needs to change?

I feel it's more about incremental steps of self-revelation. Peeling off the onion rings. Increasing vulnerability. In the place of numbness. I realize that as long as we find our way to live with integrity, strip the deceit and strive for authenticity in our lives , be mindful of our behaviour as we relate with others, and develop deeper consciousness of who we are in each moment; we can evolve to be the person in every essence we truly are and meant to be.

We can then relate to others in ways that release them to be and live the luminous lives they too are.

While this may seem complex in the way we practice living, tiptoeing around our realities, adding layers of interpretations to what's in plain sight, in truth, the simpler we make our everyday explanations the easier they are to access and engage across the experiences we create for ourselves and others. And here's the shocker. We can guarantee mistakes!! But you see, that's how we are too... Flawed yet precious. Flawed in our human-ness, Precious in the divinity of our dreams and aspirations nurtured within

LEADERSHIP IMPERATIVES
Living & Leading Beyond 2020

The landscape of the world has changed dramatically since Covid-19 hit our lives. This is perhaps the most Metamorphic Transformation of the world we have ever witnessed in our lifetime. Stories shall be told about these days throughout history. We are part of those stories. They are about how we stood up and were counted. How lives and livelihood were protected and promoted. How business design and strategy evolved to reshape and reframe the future. And how Leadership emerged from the darkness of the Lockdown to shine brightly in the sky.

Like the Sun. Burning away inequalities and inequities of the past, and growing a planet of people determined to survive, thrive and flourish, together! This book is about how that can happen. These are the pages which describe the making of this New Earth History!

This History of our Future, as chronicled in these pages is written with a Vision of the unfolding of time. As it is read, it comes to life, and builds the case for a reimagined look at Leadership beyond the Lockdown across 3 Parts of a living chronicle : Landscapes of Change, New Scripts driving Success which embrace "Now and Disruptive Change" being life partners and Leadership Imperatives which focus on Four Glorious Leaders or Leadership Personas

In particular, The Warrior Leader is an absorbing tale of Strong Goal Oriented Leadership, using the aspects of PURCHASE to put it together. Rainbow Reasoning is a remarkable rewriting of strategic decision making, really new to thinking beyond the established Black, White & Grey ways of the past. History is being rewritten with the full spectrum of Colour.

No doubt Digital Leadership will take center stage and as predicted in this book shall dominate most business conversations and strategies for the entire foreseeable future. Yet EQ Savvy Leadership and Spirit Centered Leadership must keep the heart and soul of leadership invested in people, in what can become a runaway artificially intelligent insular, clinically efficient and de-humanized world.

Reading this book not only informs us about the future of times to come, but creates the future with the turn of each page ! Enjoy your part in living and rewriting the History of the World !

THE WARRIOR LEADER

INSPIRE. INFLUENCE. IGNITE

Dexter Valles

THE WARRIOR LEADER
INSPIRE.INFLUENCE.IGNITE

This book looks at life through the eyes of leadership. A leadership with a special style. Not just to lead with, but to live with. This is the Warrior Leader. Fierce. Focused. Courageous. Competent. Compassionate. And importantly, Visionary. Versatile. Resilient. Ignited. Agile.

A Lethal array of Arrows in the Warrior Leader's Quiver. To pierce through the darkness and storm of turbulence, chaos and disruption. To reach the distant verdant hills of a flourishing life-scape which hold the heart of hope that yearns to beat once again in the bosom of humanity.

The Warrior Leader is an absorbing tale of Strong Goal Oriented Leadership, leveraging Four Attributes : Visionary, Versatile, Resilient, and Lethal

These Four Attributes are innate to a Warrior Leader. Almost like the DNA Genetic Code of such leaders. They often operate unconsciously from these when faced with crisis or crisis like circumstances. You can sense the energy radiate around a Warrior Leader and will find yourself bathed in that aura. Nothing seems too difficult or desperate when a Warrior Leader leads the way.

It's now time to realize that that very magic lies within each one of us. The Warrior Leader lives in each one of us. This book helps you create your very own Agile Warrior Leader's Battlefield Blueprint.

5 FLAGS OF LIFE
The Essence of Living & Leading Today

The Flag is probably the oldest symbol of identity, representation, honour, pride, presence and conquest. It has been used for various reasons ever since the time it was first raised as a military symbol and as a representation of national identity.

The Flag has been used to communicate both the tangible and intangible in everyday conversation. You would have used it often enough yourself. To Unfurl the Flag as a symbol of pride, hope and unique identity, to Plant the Flag in conquest, to Fly the Flag in defiance , bravado, mastery or even to surrender, to Raise the Flag on issues, to Flag Off a race, to Salute the Flag with Respect, to Keep the Flag Flying in continuous mastery and dominance.

The 5 Flags of Life are each of these and all of these. Each Flag is a symbol of your growing identity, prowess, pride, hope, dominance, mastery, conquest, respect.

Plant, Raise, Unfurl, Fly and Salute each Flag to create your unique identity and presence in life.

And finally, design your very own flag ! One which emblazons your identity with pride, for the world to recognize and acknowledge.

Made in the USA
Columbia, SC
23 October 2022

69882051R00087